Write a Western in 30 Days

With Plenty of Bullet Points!

Write a Western in 30 Days

With Plenty of Bullet Points!

Nik Morton

**COMPASS
BOOKS**

Winchester, UK
Washington, USA

First published by Compass Books, 2013
Compass Books is an imprint of John Hunt Publishing Ltd., Laurel House, Station Approach,
Alresford, Hants, SO24 9JH, UK
office1@jhpbooks.net
www.johnhuntpublishing.com
www.compass-books.net

For distributor details and how to order please visit the 'Ordering' section on our website.

ISBN: 978 1 78099 591 5

A CIP catalogue record for this book is available from the British Library.

Design: Stuart Davies

Printed and bound by CPI Group (UK) Ltd, Croydon, CR0 4YY

We operate a distinctive and ethical publishing philosophy in all
areas of our business, from our global network of authors to
production and worldwide distribution.

CONTENTS

Author's note:
I would like to express my thanks to Gill Jackson and Robert Hale Ltd for kind permission to use extracts from my novel *The $300 Man*. While these extensive extracts have been used to highlight certain aspects of writing a western, certain plot points, events and the ending have not been divulged.

Dedication

To Jennifer, my wife, best friend, and exceptional critic, with love.

To Hannah, Farhad and Darius, with love.

Author's credentials

Nik Morton is the author of the crime thriller *Pain Wears No Mask*, soon to be re-released as *The Bread of Tears*; two psychic spy Cold War thrillers *The Prague Manuscript* and *The Tehran Transmission*, soon to be re-released as *The Prague Documents* and *The Tehran Documents*, respectively; a collection of 21 crime short stories that feature Leon Cazador, *Spanish Eye*; a modern vigilante crime thriller, *A Sudden Vengeance Waits*; a vampire crime thriller, *Death is Another Life*, and an anthology in aid of the Japanese earthquake/tsunami survivors, *When the Flowers are in Bloom*. As Robin Moreton, he's the author of a World War I thriller – *Assignment Kilimanjaro*. He was commissioned to write a novel in the Cash Laramie western series, and this has garnered good reviews – *Bullets for a Ballot*.

Writing as Ross Morton, Nik has five western novels published: *Death at Bethesda Falls, Last Chance Saloon, The $300 Man, Blind Justice at Wedlock* and *Old Guns*.

He's the editor of *A Fistful of Legends*, 21 stories of the Old West. He is a member of Western Fictioneers.

He sold his first story in 1971 and has had 120 short stories published – some winning awards – in various genres, among them action, adventure, romance, ghost, horror, sci-fi, western and crime. While serving in the Royal Navy, he was a student of a writing correspondence course and was so successful he was invited to become a tutor, but his naval career commitments precluded him accepting that job.

For over forty years, he has edited periodicals and contributed hundreds of articles, book and film reviews. He has chaired several writers' circles and run writing and screenplay workshops. Since 1995, he has edited books and, for the period 2003–2007, he was sub-editor of the monthly colour magazine, *Portsmouth Post*.

In February 2011, Nik was hired as Editor in Chief of Solstice Publishing.

Nik lives in Spain with his wife Jennifer. His daughter, Hannah, son-in-law Farhad, and grandson Darius live nearby.

Introduction

Why write a western?

Received wisdom would have us believe that the western genre is dead. It died in the 1970s, buried by detective and spy fiction that swamped the market. Though seriously wounded after a few skirmishes, in fact it didn't die, because there was a renaissance in the late 1980s. But then after that western books fell into disfavour yet again... The western had a foot in Boot Hill, it seemed. That might have been the rumour a few years ago, but it would appear that, to paraphrase Mark Twain, the reports of the western's death were exaggerated. Over the last couple of years, there's been a definite resurgence in the western.

Go online and check out the number of western novels available, particularly new authors and books, and you'll be surprised at the sheer volume. Western authors have embraced the digital age. Before the release of *Stagecoach* in 1939, there'd been a slump in western movies; that film's Oscar-winning success spurred on more films in the genre. So popularity of the western rises and falls. Now, more western films are being made than for many a year. The critical sniping at Spielberg's *Cowboys & Aliens* didn't do it any harm at the box office: the film is seventh in the list of top grossing western movies; *Dances with Wolves* is still top.

Before *Avatar* and *Star Wars* ('cowboys in space') there was John Carter, the ex-Confederate Captain created by Edgar Rice Burroughs; Carter begins his adventure prospecting for gold in the Old West and ultimately finds untold wealth, love and a new planet, Barsoom (Mars). The unjustly maligned film actually did the book *A Princess of Mars* (1912) justice. Burroughs joined the 7th US Cavalry in 1896, at Fort Grant. Several westerns followed his successful Tarzan books.

At the time of writing, independent filmmakers are embracing the genre, too. *Meek's Cutoff* has achieved critical and audience acclaim. Other film projects upcoming include Johnny Depp, Quentin Tarantino, Val Kilmer, and Luke Perry being involved in different movies. Meryl Streep, Tommy Lee Jones and Hilary Swank are on-board for a new movie, *The Homesman*. And there's a string of 2012 TV westerns – *Hell on Wheels*, *Goodnight for Justice*, *Gateway*, *Hatfields & McCoys*, *Hangtown* and *Longmire*.

In the UK, Robert Hale Ltd has been publishing westerns since 1937, and the Black Horse Western imprint since the mid-1980s, and has a strong showing even today – up to eight new hardback titles per month. Many of these titles go on to Large Print editions, earning their authors additional royalties, and of course then there's the Public Lending Right annual payment, too. The PLR tends to lend credence to the assertion that westerns are still popular. My first western novel for Hale is five years old, and over that time it has been borrowed at least 5,800 times and counting – that's almost 6,000 readers of a single western. So, there is a readership out there.

Welshman Gary Dobbs, a taxi driver and bit-part actor, has penned to date five westerns under the penname Jack Martin. His first, *The Tarnished Star* (2009), was the fastest-selling Hale western ever, and a bestseller.

Alfred Wallon is a German writer; he recently signed with a publisher to write four more westerns in two on-going series. American James Reasoner is a prolific writer of crime and western novels and produces half a dozen western novels every year. Indeed, a great many crime novelists write westerns as well, among them Bill Pronzini, Bill Crider and Elmore Leonard. Many of Leonard's books have been filmed, including *Hombre*, *3:10 to Yuma* and *Valdez is Coming*.

Now, with the ubiquitous e-books, westerns are read – and written – worldwide. Westerns are produced by writers living in

New Zealand, Australia, Japan, Spain, UK, Germany, Canada and the US.

So you don't have to be an American to write a western. And that's been the case for a long time, too. Prolific author J.T. Edson published over a hundred westerns, covering nine series characters between the 1960s and 1980s. In the 1970s and 1980s, a group of British writers met at a Piccadilly pub and developed a number of western series. The group became known as the Piccadilly Cowboys; between them, they produced over three hundred of the most violent westerns ever published. Terry Harknett, Mike Linaker, Angus Wells, Ken Bulmer, Laurence James, John Harvey and Fred Nolan came up with the names of Adam Steele, Josiah Hedges, Jubal Cade, Cuchillo Oro and many more while huddled together in the pub.

The website Tainted Archive regularly runs Wild West events, encouraging bookstores around the UK and worldwide to participate.

The fourth Saturday in July is the National Day of the Cowboy in the US.

Relevance of the western

Many westerns' elemental and compelling narrative appeal may be due to that sense of the endless possibilities of adventure for the hero and heroine. There's always some new excitement along the trail, over the next ridge.

Westerns these days come in many guises. Long ago, the western escaped its straitjacket of men in white and black hats shooting it out. Of course, there's gunplay and death, but that was an aspect of the Old West, though not as commonplace as we're led to believe. Yet modern western novels can contain so much more.

Revenge is the staple plot for much Renaissance drama and of the Victorian melodrama. Revenge is a sure-fire motive for a western and there have been scores of books and films that have dealt with the subject. Yet there are still plenty of inventive variations on this age-old theme. The revenge is often driven by the hero's sense of personal honour, an inner compulsion rather than an external threat. We'll discuss the Code of the West later.

It's always refreshing to read humorous western tales, whether that's dark irony or off-the-wall slapstick; there's never enough humour, apparently. *Blazing Saddles* still sells well as a DVD, almost forty years after its release.

Unscrupulous builders, politicians and bankers are not new, even if they're in the news these days; their type figured in the Old West too.

The Old West was not tamed solely by men, of course. Women played their significant part and are often major characters in modern versions of the Old West. Women in the western represent the alternative to violence. There's a paradox here, as civilization depends on there being men who will not choose the seductive comforts the woman offers: it's as though a society without violence, a society indeed fit for women, can only come into being through violence.

Western writing is not the domain of male writers alone, and never has been; a number of female writers have produced memorable work in the field, among them Annie Proulx, Janet Dailey, Dorothy M. Johnson, Amy Sadler, and Gillian F. Taylor (the latter is a *Mastermind* finalist). Some use male pennames, such as Amos Carr, used by writer Jill McDonald-Constable, Terry James used by Joanne Walpole, Tex Larrigan, used by Irene Ord, and Terry Murphy used by Theresa Murphy. Others have opted for unisex pennames, such as M.M. Rowan and D.M. Harrison.

Every genre needs new blood, since the readership has a voracious appetite for more of the same. As it says on the cover, this guide seeks to encourage new writers to tackle the western and do so within a limited time period.

The western can cover all manner of storylines relevant to

today's readership. Dysfunctional families, domestic strife, racism, greed, crooked business, and even supernatural elements are all grist to the mill for modern writers of westerns.

Essentially, the western has a broad canvas, rich in history and imagery, a period from the 1860s to the 1890s, where myth and history intermingled. The Old West was a melting pot of nationalities, of religions, and of morality. The human condition can be examined using the mores of the western archetype. New stories of the Old West can move readers just as effectively, if not even more so, than competing genres. The only limitation is the skill of the writer.

Cliché avoidance

Remember, too, that the western genre is full of stereotypes – grizzled gunslingers, heroes who can outshoot a dozen men in the blink of an eye, shady gamblers who live by the cards and the Derringer up their sleeve, hard-faced saloon girls who have soft hearts, etc.

Some of these things may be the reason why readers are attracted to the genre. They're comfortable with the familiar. Common sense tells you that these stereotypes are not *all* that a western comprises. Filling your book with every cliché you can think of will not make it a good western.

These days, readers have certain expectations and so you should use this knowledge to surprise them. Break the mould, think laterally. Give your characters more than one dimension, a hint of realism and a personality that distinguishes them from the run-of-the-mill characters of yore. That way, readers will hopefully come back to *your* books because they're that little bit different, and not simply formulaic stories found elsewhere. (Every genre has its formulaic series of books, not just the western).

The novel's origin

What's the impetus to write a novel? It can be an idea, a phrase from a book, an incident read in a periodical, or an inspiration from some person or incident.

For *The $300 Man*, I stumbled on an interesting fact while doing research into another western. The Union draft allowed for draft dodgers – if they paid a substitute to take their place – and the going rate was $300. The title of *The $300 Man* was born.

In 1861, Andrew Carnegie, 25, invested in Columbia Oil Co. He never enlisted in the Civil War but purchased a substitute. His firm pumped 2,000 barrels a day; he also invested in the new steel industry. Two years later, at the war's height, John D. Rockefeller, 23, built with four partners an oil refinery in Cleveland near Cuyahoga River. He avoided military service by buying a substitute.

Once I had my title and the initial idea about a substitute, I then had to decide on why anyone would accept the money to go and possibly get maimed or killed. The thought of being maimed brought to mind a few heroes (and villains!) who wore a hook. I decided my hero would lose a hand in the Civil War and a hook would replace it. A special hook, however, that is adaptable for use with other tools or utensils.

You might be able to start straight in on your novel – or you may need to plot it first. That's entirely up to you. Working from a rough plot makes the going easier – and there are still usually surprises on the way to make the story interesting to you, the writer. There's a separate chapter on plot-plans.

For this novel, which would take place some years after the war, I wanted to mention $300 early on – and decided that the hero would always carry that amount – a significant reminder for him. And to create action to hook the reader, I'd have him getting robbed. These are the first words of the book, in the Prologue: The Hook:

'$300 – that'll do nicely!' said Bert Granger as he finished thumbing through the billfold Corbin Molina had been encouraged to hand over. As added persuasion, Bert held a revolver in his other hand.

'That'll do nicely' is a modern American phrase which I used for a bit of fun.

I wanted the novel to be more than a traditional western, though it would contain many of the genre's traits. As I built up the storyline, I found that it contained romance, action, betrayal, family disputes, historical events, and courage. A good mix.

The writing doesn't always go from beginning to end. That's why I use a plot-plan document. Certain scenes might pop into my head concerning particular characters – but those scenes may be further along in the story. It doesn't matter – put them into the plot-plan till you need them. Think of how films are made – scenes and characters are rarely filmed in linear fashion (usually it's for convenience and cost reduction) – the film's all slotted together in the correct order at the editing stage.

How can a book be written in 30 days?

In the days of pulp fiction, when authors were paid cents or pence per word, many genre writers produced novels in a matter of days. Among them was Jim Thompson, a crime novelist who was read by millions. Since he died, several of his books have been filmed, to considerable acclaim. Dickens was wordy because he was paid by the word. Michael Moorcock was known to write a fantasy novel in his Elric series over a weekend. Georges Simenon used to shut himself away for a couple of days and produce a Maigret novel.

Lauran Paine wrote over 900 books, among them romance, science fiction, mystery novels and hundreds of westerns, one of which was filmed as *Open Range*, starring Kevin Costner. Paine also wrote non-fiction books on the Old West, military history, witchcraft, and other subjects. Because his publishers only accepted a limited number of books under a single author's name, he adopted dozens of pseudonyms.

Since 1965, the phenomenal Jory Sherman has published over 400 novels and 500 short stories and is currently writing books in several western series for Signet and Berkley.

Writing from nine to five, five days a week, Terry Harknett, author of the Edge western series and many others, could produce a western novel in eleven days. The Edge books are being reprinted; there's a market out there, all right.

Back in 1995 I entered the One Day Novel Writing competition in London and finished joint-fourth – producing 18,000 words in two 12-hour shifts. That amounted to a novella, really, but it was still a book. In the Get Writing section I will show how you can produce about 2,000 words a day.

My first western took me a total of 19 days from conception to completion. Subsequent westerns have taken me a little longer, but not much. If I combine all five, they actually average out at well under 30 days per book.

In the old days, say the 1950s and 1960s, most genre novels ran to about 156 to 180 pages – 50,000 words or thereabouts. They were designed for a quick visceral read and had no pretensions to being great literature. Books to entertain. That's still true today, though perhaps the readership is more knowledgeable and exacting in its expectation now. Many film scripts have been based on genre fiction – the pulp length lends itself to the constraints of movie scripting. A film script doesn't contain many words, has lots of white space and usually runs to about 120 pages. My film script for my vampire crime thriller *Death is Another Life* (2011) came to 22,500 words, while the book word count was 80,000.

Most genre westerns will be about 40–45,000 words in length, though they might possibly stretch up to 60,000. If they're longer, then they probably fall into a category other than western genre, for example Historical or Saga fiction. This book is intended to encourage you to write a western genre novel of about 40–45,000 words.

Speed of production should not compromise quality of the work. If you follow my guidelines, you will still be able to produce a good quality piece of fiction – without investing a year or more in it.

The main thing to remember is that a novel requires:

- commitment,
- discipline,
- effort.

Still, it should be possible to sustain all that over a 30-day period. While the 30 days don't have to be consecutive, it will help if you can write every day for that period, as you will find yourself being carried along by the characters and the flow of the narrative. However, the choice is yours. It can be one day a week, for thirty weeks, if that's all you can manage.

The first priority is to prepare yourself.

2

Preparation

Write that story straight away!

Don't – don't dive in and start writing that novel.

There are storytellers and there are writers. Storytellers can tell a good yarn, but very few can write a cohesive, dramatic, page-turning fiction book without strong editorial help. Professional writers learn through experience and time and know what's required to keep the readers' attention. A writer who has been published *might* be called an author.

But which one are you?

It doesn't matter, really. All types may blend and merge. It's all semantics.

But what each one of them has to do is plan before beginning that novel. Even those writers who say they don't plan a book, and don't know where it will lead when they start out, they too have a plan for that beginning at the very least. Whether they like it or not, their subconscious is planning and plotting, though hopefully not towards the same end as can be found in Stephen King's *The Dark Half* (1989).

Some writers are quite happy to start with an idea, let characters enter the tale at random and stir the pot to see what happens. That works for them – but there's no guarantee that the method will lead to a finished book. Others write a first draft, then a second, and a third, until it feels right, and then stop. That works for them – but it's wasteful of time.

There's no right way to write a novel. There are plenty of wrong ways, of course. The chances are high that if you embark on your western without a plot-plan, you won't complete it in thirty days.

The army's adage is worth bearing in mind: Proper Planning

and Preparation Prevents Piss Poor Performance.

Study the market.

Whether you like it or not, your writing is aimed at a market – not the western readership, but the publisher or acquisitions editor. There are several companies who publish westerns, but not as many as there used to be. When Matt Braun published his writing guide for western novels in 1988, there was that renaissance of the western occurring and many publishing houses printed westerns. Now, over two decades later, there are fewer publishing houses thanks to mergers, amalgamations and takeovers. Inevitably, the western genre market has shrunk. So, you don't have that much choice.

In the old days, if you failed at the first hurdle (publisher), there were quite a few others available to send your rejected manuscript on to. Now, you have to hone that manuscript almost to the requirements of a particular publisher. If it fails there, you may have to consider rewriting for another publisher before sending out the book again. Whatever you do, if it fails, don't ditch it; try all avenues and if it fails, sit on it until a later date, when either the market might be more receptive or you're able to review the book with fresh critical eyes.

A good writer can get published in almost any field. They've studied their craft of storytelling and know the requirements implicit in each particular form. Less accomplished writers might contemplate trying a western, as it seems 'easier than a contemporary detective novel'. That approach is unlikely to work. To write a western, you need to have a strong affection for the genre. You don't have to be a fan, but you should respect its roots. If you don't, then it will show in the prose and storyline – and it will get rejected pronto.

First priority, then, is to identify a publisher who is currently publishing westerns. Select a handful of westerns from that publisher – ideally, not reprints of older works, but new fiction.

The selection can be from your local library or from an online book outlet, such as Amazon or The Book Depository (the latter mails books post-free anywhere in the world).

To provide variety and broaden your scope, select a number of authors rather than one.

Once you have those three or four westerns in front of you, approach the reading in a business-like manner. Analyse each book as you read it. Make many notes. This is not to slavishly copy but to get a feel for the structure, vocabulary, pace, number of characters in a published western.

For example, what is the author's approach to the readers? Do the books from this publisher possess an ethos? There are a couple of Christian publishers of westerns, for instance. Is the message open and obvious or subtle?

Even though it's fiction, what kind of topics and facts are used in the book? And to what depth are they treated?

Are there any subjects that appear to be taboo?

What kind of title does the publisher/author favour? A word, a phrase, a sentence? A question, a statement, an exclamation? A play on words or simply serious? How many words are usually in the title?

The following questions to pose don't have to be applied to the whole book, that would be tedious, but study several pages to get a feel for the style, presentation and variety in the prose. For example: How many lines of dialogue per page? What age and status are the characters? How many paragraphs to each chapter? What is the usual number of words in the paragraphs? Are the sentences all a similar length or do they vary? What marks of punctuation are used?

What kind of vocabulary is used? Simple, or moderately educated or really literary?

Study the first paragraph. How does it appeal to the reader? Is there any special emphasis on topicality, conflict or emotion? Remember, it is the first five words that attract the casual reader's eye; so these should be especially striking. Try to avoid opening with 'A', 'The', 'It' or 'There'.

In the final paragraph, how is the book wound up? Is it satisfactory?

Some book blurbs use quotations from the novel as teasers. Study these snippets – they're like sound bites, there to suck in the browsing reader. Does your work contain similar phrases or sentences that could be gainfully used to 'sell' your story? (I know, you haven't written the book yet – but consider identifying appropriate sound bites as your writing approaches the end of the book).

How many chapters does each book contain? Picked at random, four books I'm now looking at have, respectively, 15, 10, 16 and 20 chapters. Many beginning writers worry about the number of chapters, but there's no need. A chapter break can be made almost anywhere – to signify the passing of time, to leave the reader wanting more after a cliffhanger situation, to foreshadow worse to come. In fact, deciding on chapter breaks can wait until the self-edit stage.

Westerns are invariably about action – but not exclusively so. One of these four novels has a fight (fist or gun) in seven of the fifteen chapters. Another has seven fights in twenty-one chapters.

So, study the pacing and the relevant vocabulary.

Vocabulary

Perhaps more than any other, the western has a wealth of words particular to its genre.

Remember, though, that you're not striving to throw in as many typical words and phrases as possible in order to impress or win points. The vocabulary should arise from the characters and the situation – *and* the time period.

Avoid anachronisms. Decide on the period you're writing about (preferably the month or months, as well as the year) and ensure that the guns and clothing you describe are appropriate for that date. For example, blue denim Levis were not available until after 1873, and the Stetson wasn't around before 1865.

If you're going to have characters travel by stagecoach, then remember that the first transcontinental stage line was begun by Butterfield's Overland Mail Company in 1858. Ben Holladay's Overland Stage Line dates from 1864 – and was amalgamated into Wells, Fargo in 1866. Yes, the name *Wells, Fargo* has a comma – though some writers often drop it.

The first-ever Wild West Show was in 1870 – and it was a flop. Wild Bill Hickok collected together three cowboy ropers, six buffalo, four Comanche Indians, a performing bear and a monkey. The buffalo wouldn't perform, the bear hibernated, and box office receipts nose-dived. The Comanche threatened to scalp their boss if they weren't paid. So the buffalo were sold to a butcher to pay the Indians' wages and Hickok left for Kansas to tame Hays City.

A horse isn't just a horse. There are a lot of types – so try to vary them, whether it's a roan, broomtail, bay, buckskin, or a chestnut. In Andy Adams' novel (q.v.), he lists the ten mounts he was allocated from the cattle drive's remuda: three sorrels, two greys, a black, two coyotes, a brown and a grulla. You'll encounter all kinds in your sample selection, I'm sure.

Clothing – identify how much description is given over to what characters wear. Clothing helps the reader visualise the character – more on that in Chapter 11.

Geography – does the writer convey a sense of place? And how is it done? Usually, it should be accomplished only with judicious and selective prose. This isn't a travelogue, after all; it's a western.

Some regular words and phrases picked up from those four books I analysed:

False fronts

Arroyo – a dry narrow gully – flooded during times of flash floods

Boardwalk

Levi's pants

Gold coin – double eagle

Coffee – java or Arbuckle's

Airtights – cans (of food, such as peaches)

Sawbones – doctor

Barkeep – bar tender

Hogleg – revolver

Opined – thought

Cayuse – horse, maybe wild

Mackinaw – heavy blanket or plaid coat made from a blanket

Chaps – protection from cactus or barbed wire, rope burns etc. From the Spanish *chaparreras*, offering protection against chaparral

Soiled dove – calico queen, scarlet lady, prostitute/dance hall girl

Wanted dodger – wanted poster

Quirley – roll-your-own cigarette, often with Bull Durham tobacco

Whiskey – raw alcohol with names such as Forty-Rod, Tarantula Juice, Red Eye and Coffin Varnish.

This isn't a tick-off list for you to use in your own book. Rather, it's intended to illustrate the richness of the language available in a western. Researching the lingo for yourself will help immerse you in the genre, all the better to write about the Old West. But, as already mentioned, don't overdo it. Create the flavour; don't swamp the prose.

Phrasing

Highlight or make a note of any phrasing that catches your eye or imagination. You won't copy it for your own purposes, of course, but perhaps it can be adapted or paraphrased. Perhaps a taciturn fellow would be referred to, thus: 'He doesn't say much. He saves his breath for breathing.'

Another random expression is 'Got sand in his craw' – which means a brave fellow.

In addition to those sample books, study some non-fiction books of the period and analyse the manner of speech and description.

Western lore

Here's a very brief sample of information I've gleaned, but there's much more than this waiting to be discovered.

'Always tend to your horse's needs before your own' is a credo most of your cowboys should follow. In the livery, the horse should get a nosebag of grain and a rub down and some hay. And that's before the rider seeks sustenance for himself. To quote Andy Adams, 'No better word can be spoken of a man than that he is careful of his horses.'

Saddle-sore lore. The bedroll was tied behind the cantle of the saddle, while the canteen was slung over the saddle horn. The cinch was the girth and needed to be tightened; woe betide a tenderfoot if he let the animal blow himself up against the girth, so that when the horse let out its breath, the saddle capsized with the rider on-board! Saddles should be oiled at least once a year. The saddle scabbard or boot held the man's rifle. Some riders roweled their horses, which often suggested the man's mean or unkind nature. Generally, large dull rowels were the type commonly used, according to Andy Adams (q.v. Chapter 3, Research).

And of course there were different types of saddles, depending on where the rider originated or worked: Spanish, double cinch, centerfire and Porter saddle No. 78. The saddle had to be comfortable for the horse, too; if the saddle was a poor fit, a horse's back could become painfully raw. Indeed, cowboys were fired from their jobs for 'beefsteaking' their mounts.

When the weather reflected a serious drop in the mercury, cowboys would take their horse's bridle to bed with them, so that the bit wouldn't freeze the animal's tongue in the morning.

The *New York Tribune* was used as wallpaper and homesteaders thought nothing of 'reading the walls' to occupy themselves.

Purge, puke and bleed. That's what many medics advocated with their camphor, calomel, castor oil and other cathartics.

Illustration by excerpt

From time to time, throughout this book I'll insert various excerpts from my western *The $300 Man* to illustrate certain points.

For this purpose, I'll outline the main characters here, since their names will crop up before the chapter about building characters.

The $300 Man characters

Corbin Molina, half Mexican, half Anglo, with a hook in place of his missing left hand.

Samuel Walker, the powerhouse of Walkerville

Lydia Walker, Sam's strong-willed mother

Malinda Dix, a female doctor

Jean Pegram, an old flame of Corbin's

Granger siblings, out-and-out villains: Bert, Elijah, Arnold and Stella

Deshler, the sheriff of the town of Retribution

Joe Tillman, a gunslinger and gun for hire

Mae Begley, the madam of Heaven's Gateway bordello

Ready to begin

At the end of this preparation, when you've amassed sufficient knowledge to be familiar with the style and content of several western novels, you're ready.

So start the spreadsheet.

But what do you put on the spreadsheet?

Set a word count target – for example: 45,000 (This enables you to calculate the number of words you have left to write – column F below).

Each row:

Column A: Number of days for the project/book, beginning with 1

Column B: Date

Column C: Start time for session

Column D: End time for session

Column E: Word count at the end of the day (or each session if more than one session per day, when broken down into hours of work)

Column F: Words left – the sum (45,000 minus today's word count) [=SUM (45000 minus E column)]

Column G: Words per day – the sum of (today's word count (E) minus the previous day's word count (E on previous row)).

Column H: Hours per day/session

For example:

A	B	C	D	E	F	G	H
				TOTAL	LEFT	PER DAY	HRS
1	Prelim			1982	43018		
2	1 Apr	17:30	19:30	3545	41455	1563	2
3	7 Apr	18:00	19:30	4521	40479	976	1.5
4	12 Apr	13:30	14:30	5722	39278	1201	1
5	14 Apr	15:00	16:00	7430	37570	1708	1

It cannot be overemphasized, the spreadsheet is crucial to

attaining your goal of writing the novel in 30 days. The spread-sheet will keep you on track. It will goad you on and encourage you. As the word count mounts, you'll find your narrative pace quickening.

The 'words per day' count will show you your good and bad days. For one of my books, the daily word count varied from 164 words for one day to 2,179.

Indeed, towards the end it's quite possible, during the self-edit phase, that the word count might be in minus figures. One day, I had a word count of minus 144 as I tightened prose and cut out unnecessary words!

How do you measure 30 days?

Good question. Nobody can write solidly for twenty-four hours. It has to depend on the time you have available to you. A so-called normal working day is supposed to be eight hours in length. True, some occupations require more than that. At sea, I often worked a fourteen-hour day. And then there was that One Day Novel Writing competition, with my two twelve-hour sessions.

You might have heard of the NaNoWriMo – the annual National Novel Writing Month. Writers can sign up to write 50,000 words of a novel in a month. It doesn't have to be of publishable quality; it's supposed to be the first draft. Hundreds of writers complete this marathon every year, while others fall by the wayside; and from these completed attempts spring, eventually, fully fledged novels. That's intense, because it is literally over a 30-day period.

You need to be sensible about your work allocation, or you'll be tempted to cheat yourself and then give up when your target isn't met.

I'd advocate keeping track by 'signing-in' on your spreadsheet and 'signing-out' when you finish any particular session. Clock-in on the spreadsheet with a start-time and then close down with an end-time, as shown in the table above.

Measure your 'day' when you've hit those eight hours.

As can be seen from the example spreadsheet above, although the writing shown took place from 1 April to 14 April, the actual hours spent on the book only amounted to 5.5; so there were still 2.5 hours left in that first 'day'.

In essence, then, your 30 days' work amounts to 240 hours. Plenty of time!

3

Research

At risk of stating the obvious, all Old West fiction is historical fiction. Any historical fiction relies on research. Unless you're an expert on the period, you'll need to do some research. And even if you're an expert, check your facts, as memory can be cruelly deceptive.

It doesn't have to be a great amount of research; otherwise you'll spend all your time reading background tomes and won't write any fiction.

What you glean from research is there to impart verisimilitude. You're not only going to write about what happened in that period – but, more importantly, why. It's often the 'why' that motivates the characters. Your research also helps mould the story and characters with insights from true life. And it can suggest fresh subplots and character situations, too.

How much research do I do?

Sufficient for your story. But don't skimp – respect your reader. Remember, the Wild West was only a brief moment in history – roughly from 1865 to 1900, some thirty-five years. Granted, there's been overlap to pre-Civil War and early 1900s, but on the whole most western genre fiction falls into that thirty-five-year bracket.

The place of the Wild West is sometimes defined west of the Mississippi, too – though that doesn't take into account flashbacks elsewhere. My long short story 'Silence' featured in the anthology *The Traditional West* takes place in the 1890s Old West; yet it has flashbacks to 1858 in New York, when some Italian immigrants arrived, and it also covered the draft riots of 1863 and the gangs that evolved in Gotham.

So you can't just decide on your period as being the 1880s. Nail that date – and by so doing, you're immediately putting some welcome limit on your research. Your main theme and subject will also come into clearer perspective once you have a fixed date in mind.

If you have a small reference library on the period, and the action in your book is taking place in a town and the saloon figures highly, then grab that book and turn to the Index for information about saloons. If you don't have the books yet, that's not a problem, these days. Target your search on Google to pull up information on saloons in the Old West.

You need to be selective, as you'll be surprised how much detail you'll quickly amass, whether it's the type of liquor served or the kind of card games played.

At the end of this chapter I've listed a selection of useful books you might wish to consider for your reference library. Also, I've included some useful links to Internet resources.

Just the Facts, Ma'am

It's so easy to become wrapped up in the interesting facts in your research. The danger is not only spending time on them rather than writing, but also in extracting too much information. Yes, it's fascinating, but is it all pertinent to the story and the characters? Does it help move the story forward? Probably not.

Of course, this doesn't stop some authors who commit that annoying sin of lumbering their readers with the dreaded 'infodump' – literally, paragraph upon paragraph of fact, information gleaned during research that the author considers so interesting that you're bound to want to know all about it too. Sure, some bestsellers do it – but you aren't a bestseller, so be kind to your reader and avoid falling into the infodump trap. Really, infodumping is lazy writing. Be circumspect with the research details you use.

Naturally, you want to divulge the pertinent facts in some

manner. Not as cold author intrusive text. Preferably via character exposition, and *not* directly in the narrative. Even here, you have to tread carefully. Some authors think if they disguise their infodump text in dialogue, it will be all right. Not so. It still seems stilted, unreal and declares that the author was too indolent to weave the research material into the fabric of the story.

The $300 Man research

Once I'd decided that Corbin and Malinda would like poetry, I had to find poets that were contemporary with the time. My first thought was Emily Dickinson, but a little research gleaned that her works, though written at that time, were published after 1873. So I settled on Christina Rossetti. I already knew Whitman was contemporaneous with the Civil War. Although it's unlikely to apply, beware of quoting poets who haven't been dead for 70 years – they're still in copyright.

After the end of the Civil War (1865), the Bureau of Refugees, Freedmen and Abandoned Lands was set up to aid distressed refugees. Although intended to last only a year, the bureau continued its work long after that, as there was a strong need to aid former slaves through education, health care and employment, an important aspect of the Reconstruction of the South. By 1871, however, enthusiasm for the bureau waned and funds dried up. Anyway, for many years, freedmen – ex-slaves – were exploited, so in my book Walker becomes one of those men to exploit them – and the Mexicans.

Reconstruction of the South. Certain northerners moved south during Reconstruction, between 1865 and 1877, to reform, take economic advantage and dominate the politics of the southern states. As they tended to travel using carpetbags, they were nicknamed carpetbaggers. Not all so-called carpetbaggers were conmen or on the make.

I used some of this research in the scene at p. 91, when Corbin is talking to Tillman:

> Corbin nodded. 'You know as well as I that we Yankees started to flood the southern states as soon as the war was over. Reformers, carpetbaggers, teachers, businessmen, some of them full of missionary ideals, plenty more just looking for easy pickings. The south was reeling, its businesses bust, its men exhausted or dead.'
>
> 'Sure. Many a plantation changed hands for piffling sums. I reckon it was a mite unsavoury, the hasty way they went about it.'

Even this exposition has a purpose – it creates a bond of respect between the two men.

In the story, the silver mine is a contentious issue between the Mexicans and Walker. I needed to do research on the silver mining process of that time, particularly as I'd thought of having the denouement in the mine. I played with the description when Corbin is taken captive on p. 144:

> Over to their right was a big compound, where rail lines ran from the mine. Within the compound, Corbin knew, would be several shallow-walled enclosures, filled with ore and the processing mixture, perhaps a layer two feet deep. Beyond was the corral where they kept the horses that plodded round the big tubs, moving paddles to mix the ingredients – salt, water, *magistral* and mercury. Now it was quiet, though a bitter metallic smell lingered in the air.

Weapons

If it's a western, then guns of one type or another are surely going to appear. Really, it's no good just writing about six-guns or rifles. Readers of westerns expect a bit more than that. Besides, if you want the story to appear as real as you can make it, you must opt for the particular over the general. Sure, many readers might not be able to distinguish between a Navy Colt and a Peacemaker, but they're more likely to believe you since you mention them specifically. As you will note in Chapter 8 – Character Creation, I've listed the weapons that the main characters carry.

Beware of anachronisms, of course. Don't have a character using a weapon before its time of availability. Cap and ball percussion revolvers were superseded in the early 1870s by guns that took cartridge ammunition. The cap and ball reload was a long process so some of these revolvers came with removable cylinders which could be pre-loaded – as seen notably in the Clint Eastwood film *Pale Rider*.

There's a little confusion over the favourite weapon used by gamblers. Henry Deringer designed and produced a small single-shot muzzle-loading large-bore cap-lock pistol long before William Elliot designed the small double-barreled breach-loading large-bore cartridge pistol known as the Derringer. The Deringer (one 'r') was built by Henry prior to the Civil War, while the Derringer (double 'r') was built by Remington after the war.

The Peacemaker was notoriously slow to load: it had to be brought to half-cock, the loading gate opened, and then each chamber ejected and reloaded in turn, while the cylinder was rotated 1/6-turn between each unload/load. Hence the men who carried two guns, one being a spare where a reload was required in a hurry.

Remember, most who carried the Peacemaker left the top chamber empty, to avoid accidentally firing the weapon: the firing pin rests on the primer of the cartridge in line with the barrel and the slightest knock could fire it. More than enough historical reports testify to cowboys accidentally shooting themselves, usually in the foot, by not keeping that chamber empty.

Clothing

Again, try to go beyond 'a blue dress', 'a pin-stripe suit' for the apparel your main characters wear. It doesn't take much research to latch on to a few variations. The reader doesn't want a detailed fashion report, but the occasional appropriate reference adds colour and believability. The character list should be where you note the various types of clothing worn by your characters.

Wearing his best dark blue silk coat and vest, complete with ochre cravat and silver tie-clip, he felt sure that this time Mrs Walker would look kindly on him. (p 38)

She sat opposite him and her mauve dress set off her golden brown complexion. Her sleeves were short and puffed, while the scooped neckline flirted with the swell of her breasts. Corbin thought that Dr Malinda Dix looked every inch the Southern lady with her flounced skirt trimmed with ruches. (p 132)

Beware of inappropriate references for the period. Apparently, it was the hot summer in the early 1890s that drove some men to stop wearing braces and opt for belts, so belts for keeping up trousers were not commonplace before then. In fact, Levi Strauss didn't put belt loops on his jeans until the 1920s. Levis arrived on the range in the 1850s and were made of canvas, but he soon switched to the more pliable denim.

Shirts generally worn by cowboys were tough and sweat-absorbent heavy flannel or wool.

Besides the Stetson already mentioned, other hats worn were the ten-gallon hat, the Montana peak, sombreros and the Texas hat. There were many local variations in the way crowns were creased and the angles at which brims were set.

Cooking

There are several resources that can supply you with the types of food eaten by people out west, from cowboys being fed at their chuck wagons to guests at a hotel. The point of research is to create a realistic image for the reader – and you can only do that by selecting the particular over the general. 'He ate his food and stepped out of the hotel' won't cut it; see this subject in Chapter 5 regarding Character POV.

Types of food are varied, some familiar, some less so:

- barbecued beef ribs,
- beef and tomato chilli,
- chicken fried steak,
- pan fried steak,
- chilli bean sandwich,
- Dutch oven pot roast,
- iron skillet potatoes,
- beans, bacon, refried beans,
- sourdough bread,
- Texan pecan cake,
- cornbread,
- sourdough flapjacks,
- omelette,
- and of course coffee.

Music

It wasn't only cowboys on the range who sang – over their campfires or to the steers at bed down time – but also vaudeville singers, male and female, who toured the townships.

So, don't neglect the existence of music – it was an important aspect of many otherwise humdrum lives.

The instruments:

- guitar,
- fiddle,
- banjo,

- harmonica,
- the Jew's harp
- and we can't leave out that staple in saloons, the upright piano.

Gambling

Saloons, mining town tents, paddle steamers, and bordellos – they might all have a gambling den of some sort. Miners and cowboys didn't have much to spend their money on and even the slim chance of winning big often sucked (suckered?) them in to a game of one sort or another. On the Internet, I pulled off the rules and actually played faro, with 'pretend money', in order to learn enough to represent the game in my novel *Last Chance Saloon*.

Cowboys weren't supposed to gamble on a cattle drive, but they did. As they didn't get paid till the end of the drive, they played for matchsticks or anything that could be used as chips, to be redeemed at trail's end. So, there's adequate cause here for a grudge or two that festers – even over the years.

A great variety of games were played in the saloons, among them:

- Faro, also called tiger. Attempting to win – 'bucking the tiger'
- Draw and stud poker, the cowmen's favourite
- Roulette, also known as rouge-et-noir and chusa
- Spanish monte
- Twenty-one, also called blackjack or vingt-et-un
- Keno
- Seven-up, no, not the drink!
- Chuck-a-luck, played with three dice, originally British
- Backgammon
- Wheel of fortune
- Craps
- Fantan, of Chinese origin

- Whist and euchre, played by staid settlers, mainly

Faro was probably the most popular card game of the period, especially with the miners. Apparently, every faro table in Soapy's Tivoli Club in Denver, Colorado was set up to cheat the gambling public. The trouble was, faro was so popular that even those who knew the game was rigged continued to play it, mainly because 'It's the only game in town' worth playing. Like most gambling, faro was considered by many as a dangerous scam that destroyed families and reduced men to poverty. Since cheating was so prevalent, that's not surprising. Just maybe, this time, the house will lose? No chance.

Code of the West

The unwritten 'code' was based on loyalty and cooperation, and any violation of the code could be severe, punishment being ostracism or even death. For example, a Yellowstone City, Montana by-law stipulated that hanging was mandatory for 'murder, thieving or for insulting a woman'. A man who dared mistreat a woman was regarded as a social pariah, which wasn't so surprising since men outnumbered women ten to one out west. A 'real' lady was held in the highest esteem, never insulted or embarrassed. It was almost entirely unknown for a young woman to become an unmarried mother. Needless to say, there were exceptions – and there have to be, in order to provide rich dramatic storylines!

Women represented the finer side of life. They were the teachers, the exemplars, the driving force behind social activities, and a constant reminder of the more comfortable, civilized lives so many men had left behind in the East.

A man's word was his bond and, as an extension of that, it was advocated that you should never abuse another man's trust, especially if the other was at a disadvantage. Honesty was the cornerstone of the cowboy's sense of honour. One ranch foreman sacked a hired hand who hadn't paid his bill to a local prostitute. The ultimate insult for a cowboy was to be ordered to turn in his horses and leave the ranch on foot.

If a person was in trouble, it was a man's duty to help him – friend, stranger or enemy.

And because of the great distances between neighbours and townships, hospitality was generous. No payment was expected; in fact, most hosts were downright insulted if it was offered. And on the other side of the coin, his neighbours loathed an inhospitable man.

On approach, a stranger would keep astride his horse in full view and call, 'Hello the house!' and he'd only dismount after being invited to come inside for warmth, victuals or coffee.

Despite the strong strain of hospitality, it was considered that another man's business was his own affair. Prying was considered bad manners, as endorsed by one wiseacre who commented, 'Minding one's own business is the best life insurance.' So, a person's past belonged to him alone, and should remain a closed book if that's how he wanted it.

The 'code' forbade shooting an unarmed man, so it made sense not to pack a pistol. However, a man whose personal sense of honour had been threatened was justified in taking a shot at the man who'd insulted him.

As already hinted at, not everyone abided by the 'code'. Most laws are sensible, to protect the weak and maintain civilisation. But not everybody stays within the law. True, there are bad laws – and this was the case in the Old West, when several individuals might protest and become outlaws.

It's useful to be aware of the existence of the 'code'. Your hero might flout some aspects yet stick to others through thick and thin: it helps you shape your hero's character traits.

Landscape
The Old West landscape is broad, covering several states and a

number of territories not yet admitted to statehood (the date they joined the United States are shown in brackets). Arkansas, Texas, California, Oregon, Kansas (1861), Nevada (1864), Nebraska (1867), Colorado (1876), North Dakota (1889), South Dakota (1889), Montana (1889), Wyoming (1890), Oklahoma (1907), New Mexico (1912) and Arizona (1912).

Each state (or independent territory) has its own geography, history of western expansion, desperadoes and heroes, all ready to be tapped by diligent research.

Several of my westerns take place in South Dakota, so I grabbed snippets of information about the flora and fauna. Here's an example from my notes:

- *Flora.* Oak, maple, beech, birch, hickory, and willow are all represented in South Dakota's forests while thickets of chokecherry, wild plum, gooseberry and currant are all found in the eastern part of the state. Pasqueflower (Anemone ludoviciana) is the state flower as of 1889; other wild flowers are beardtongue, bluebell, and monkshood.

- *Fauna.* Familiar native mammals are the coyote (the state animal, when it became a state, not before!), porcupine, raccoon, bobcat, buffalo, white-tailed and mule deer, white-tailed jackrabbit, and black-tailed prairie dog. Nearly three hundred species of birds make their home here, among them: the sage grouse, bobwhite quail, and ring-necked pheasant, which are leading game birds. There's the Eskimo curlew, least tern and the bald eagle. Fish include the trout, pallid sturgeon, catfish, pike, bass, and perch.

- *Topography.* The eastern two-fifths of South Dakota is prairie, belonging to the Central Lowlands. The western three-fifths falls within the Missouri Plateau, part of the Great Plains region; the High Plains extend into the southern fringes of the state. The Black Hills, an extension of the Rocky Mountains, occupy the southern half of the state's western border; the mountains, which tower about 4,000 ft (1,200 m) over the neighbouring plains, include Harney Peak, at 7,242 ft (2,209 m) the highest point in the state. East of the southern Black Hills are the Badlands, a barren, eroded region with extensive fossil deposits. South Dakota's lowest elevation, 966 ft (295 m), is at Big Stone Lake, in the north-eastern corner.

○ You need to be careful if using heights of mountains while your characters climb or ride up them – how does he know the height?

○ Rivers are often important story features. Flowing south and southeast, the Missouri River cuts a huge swathe through the heart of South Dakota before forming part of the south-eastern boundary. Tributaries of the Missouri include the Grand, Cheyenne, Bad, Moreau, and White rivers in the west and the James, Vermillion, and Big Sioux in the east.

Naturally, the idea is not to bombard the reader with all this information. A novel might only feature one of the birds, maybe a couple of the flowers.

If you don't want your reader's eyes to glaze over, haul back on the research information. Inject just enough for the suggestion of realism, colour and effect.

Recommended research resources

Still short of ideas? Don't worry. You will find countless story-lines and plots by simply browsing through some of your research books.

Naturally, as with any historical fiction, you can also glean much from fiction about that period. The idea is not to plagiarise, but to immerse yourself in the period of the book, and many authors do that very successfully. If your subconscious is already suitably immersed, then your story will benefit when you come to write it.

Note also that this popular historic period was photographed. You have a wonderful resource in old photos from the various towns, pictures of the gunmen and the townspeople, all to aid you in bringing your descriptions alive.

Time-Life Books – The Old West (1976)

A wealth of information in many volumes covering Trailblazers, Loggers, Gunfighters, Expressmen, Rivermen, Chroniclers, Frontiersmen, the Indians, the Scouts, Gamblers and several others.

Dictionary of the American West by Winfred Blevins (1993)

It is just what it says, and fascinating as well as invaluable.

The Prairie Traveler by Randolph B Marcy, Captain US Army (1859, reprinted 1993)

Written at the period of western expansion, with routes, details about clothing, provisions etc.

The Writer's Guide to Everyday Life in the Wild West by Candy Moulton (1999)

Covers the period 1840–1900, concerning the history, clothes, food, drink, education and so much more.

Guns of the Old West by Jeff Cooper (2008)

Reprint of original book dated 1950s. Useful, with plenty of illustrations.

How the West Was Worn by Chris Enss (2006)

'Bustles and buckskins on the wild frontier!' Covers some of the material (no pun intended) found in Candy Moulton's book, but there are also plenty of fresh snippets of information – and more illustrations.

Wondrous Times on the Frontier by Dee Brown (1991)

The author of *Bury My Heart at Wounded Knee* strips away the Hollywood façade of the Old West to reveal the truth about the lives of the pioneers, their ambition and hardship, the cruelty and humour. A feast of anecdotes.

The Encyclopaedia of the Old West by Denis McLoughlin (1977)

From Abalone to Zuni Indians, this is a fascinating compendium of characters, places and events in the Old West, spiced with wit and humour by the author who comes from Bolton, Lancashire.

Saloons of the Old West by Richard Erdoes (1979)

A fully illustrated book of fact, fable, legend and anecdote about saloons!

The Gunfighters by James D. Horan (1976)

Accounts by eyewitnesses and the gunfighters themselves, with a few gruesome photographs.

The West: The Making of the American West by Jon E. Lewis (1996)

A one-book compendium of anecdotal history and western lore, with appendices of a timeline and extensive bibliography.

The Civil War Book of Lists (Combined Books Inc., 1994)

A fascinating variety of lists, such as best commanders on both sides, casualty figures, state and ethnic origin of armies, the songs and poems, as well as some frivolous stuff – the delicacies made from hardtack, the ugliest generals and the strangest hairstyles!

Cowboys, Mountain Men and Grizzly Bears by Matthew P. Mayo (2011)

50 true tales, providing enough storylines to keep you going for a long time!

Son of the Morningstar by Evan S. Connell (1997)

A classic account of Custer and the Little Big Horn.

Roughing It by Mark Twain (1872)

Life on the Mississippi by Mark Twain (1883)

Two first-hand accounts of his travels through the west by a true wordsmith, rich in jargon of the period.

The Log of a Cowboy by Andy Adams (1903)

A classic fictional but authentic account by a cowboy. Can be downloaded from Project Gutenberg and other sources.

North American Indians by George Catlin (1867)

A classic contemporary account of Catlin's time among the Indians, with his illustrations.

The Foxfire Book edited by Eliot Wigginton and his students (1972)

Tells you about log cabin building, snake lore, mountain crafts, foods, hunting tales, and home remedies. There are eleven other books in this series about Appalachian self-sufficiency, many of which can be extrapolated to your fiction.

True West monthly magazine

'Captures the spirit of the West with authenticity, personality and humour by providing a necessary link from our history to our present.'

How to Write Western Novels by Matt Braun (1988)

Does what it says, with a few examples from Braun's and other writers' work, but doesn't go into the nitty-gritty like this book.

Writing Westerns: How to Craft Novels that Evoke the Spirit of the West by Mike Newton (Kindle) (2012)

Does what it says, with lots of lists. 'Research, talent, and imagination are the keys to writing a successful novel.'

Internet resources

At the time of writing, the following Internet links were accessible. Invariably, many of them are blogs rather than websites, and they have other links to western sites and mystery and movie sites, among others. There's no guarantee that their domain names will continue, however. This list is not exhaustive, but it should set you on the trail.

http://www.westernauthors.com – a directory of western authors.

http://www.tombstoneoldwestbooks.com/ – just what it says, a site where you can purchase books about the Old West.

http://www.thewesternonline.com/index.html –The Western

Online – Fiction, articles, reviews on the Old West by Matthew Pizzolato.

http://www.lifeintheoldwest.com/ – Life in the Old West website – true stories, tall tales and memorabilia of the American West.

http://www.piccadillypublishing.org – Piccadilly Publishing – prints new and classic western fiction, many series characters. *Not currently accepting new submissions; keep checking.*

http://henryswesternroundup.blogspot.com.es/ – Henry's Western Round-up – Weekly news about western movie and book releases.

http://www.blackhorsewesterns.com – Black Horse Extra is an informative newsletter with heaps of information about the Old West and current books, with articles by western authors. Colourful, informative, and fun.

http://blackhorseexpress.blogspot.com.es/ – Black Horse Express – Up-to-date information on all the latest Black Horse Western books, with a monthly Amazon bestseller listing and great cover images. Brief extracts and links are provided to all the news, reviews, interviews and other information that becomes available about your favourite authors.

http://www.meridianbridge.com/ – Meridian Bridge – Richard Prosch's blog of his own personal west, featuring reviews of westerns and interviews with writers of westerns.

http://brokentrails.blogspot.com – Broken Trails – The blog of Ray Foster, who has written westerns as Jack Giles. 'I was born in North London but moved to Orpington, Kent. Having brought up six children and seen them married off – as a result we now have 15 grandchildren – we have retired to the wilds of Suffolk.'

http://ijparnham.blogspot.com –The Culbin Trail – The blog of Ian Parnham. As I.J. Parnham he has written 27 novels for the Black Horse Western series and 6 for the Avalon Western series.

http://www.tantor.com/BookList.asp?Genre=Westerns&lid=ln av – audiobooks.

http://www.whiskeycreekpress.com – publisher of print and e-books, including westerns.

http://uk.groups.yahoo.com/group/westernaddictsand-drifters/ – This online e-mail community for western lovers is dedicated to the Old West in fact and fiction. Join the group to talk about historical events, films and books.

http://groups.yahoo.com/group/WesternPulps/ – Group dedicated to the western pulp magazines.

http://westerntrailblazer.com – an independent publisher of westerns in e-book and print format.

http://tainted-archive.blogspot.com.es/ – Tainted archive – Gary Dobbs has been publishing this since 2008. It covers a broad spectrum of pop culture but has a strong emphasis on westerns in books, comics and films, with author interviews and book reviews.

http://westernfictionreview.blogspot.com.es/ – Western fiction review – For years and years Steve Myall has been a reader – and collector – of western fiction, mainly from series. Sometime ago (2008) he was persuaded to write reviews and these are now appearing here. Along with these reviews you'll also find interviews with authors and cover artists.

http://buddiesinthesaddle.blogspot.com.es/ – Buddies in the saddle – the frontier west in history, myth and popular literature by Ron Scheer.

http://romancingthewest.blogspot.com – Romancing the West. Colourful, interesting interviews with western authors, hosted by Jacquie Rogers.

http://www.westernfictioneers.com/ –Western Fictioneers – An organization of professional authors of western novels and short stories. Set up in 2010. Western Fictioneers is a professional organization for authors who work in the genre of the traditional western; the western is the Great American Story, the unique history and mythology, and it remains as relevant as it ever was. Runs the annual Peacemaker Award competition.

http://westernfictioneers.blogspot.com – Official Blog of the Western Fictioneers, Professional Authors of Traditional Western Novels and Short Stories.

http://www.western-review.com/ – The Western Review was established in 2008 with the intention of providing quality reviews and information relating to as many western as possible, from Oscar winners, genre-makers and genre-breakers, to Italowesterns, American B-pictures and long lost telemovies.

http://slapbookleather.blogspot.com – Slap Bookleather – blog about the western in comics, film, TV and books.

http://spurandlock.blogspot.com – Spur and Lock – blog by Duane Spurlock. An occasional look at the west, wild and otherwise, in fiction and non-fiction, comics, moving pictures, radio, music, and in ways yet determined or created.

http://www.frontiertales.com/index.php – Frontier Tales – online magazine of new western fiction short stories.

http://groups.yahoo.com/group/FrontierTimes/ – A yahoo group where you can chat about westerns. Membership is free.

http://www.westernreference.com/ – Pat Hawk's Western Series & Sequels. Hawk's Enterprises researches, compiles, publishes and supports the finest reference books for Reference Librarians, Book Dealers and serious genre fans. Topics are selected where scarce or little information exists. Publish and continue to update the most comprehensive book on author pseudonyms for books published in the English language. Also publish series books in the Western, Science Fiction and Adventure/Intrigue genres. A Mystery series book is one of the projects in-work.

http://www.us.penguingroup.com/static/pages/features/actionwesterns/index.html – Action westerns from Penguin Books, USA

http://westernwriters.org/ – Western Writers of America Inc. Founded in 1953 to promote the literature of the American West and bestow Spur Awards for distinguished writing in the western field. The founders were largely authors who wrote traditional western fiction, but the organization swiftly expanded to include historians and other non-fiction authors, young adult and romance writers, and writers interested in regional history. Today it has over 600 members. Its annual convention occurs each June, which concludes with the Spur Awards banquet, the moment when the WWA honours those who win the coveted awards. WWA actively helps its members promote their books and articles, and aggressively promotes the literature of the American West, which it considers this country's unique contribution to world literature. Membership fee required, open to all published writers who derive their livelihood, in whole or in part, from writing about the land and the peoples of the American West, past and present.

General books on writing

Writers of westerns shouldn't just read that genre, of course. The broader their knowledge base, the more interest they can bring to their writing. Writers should never stop learning. Writing is a craft and like any other skill it has to be learned and honed with time and experience. Just because you can speak the language and have an affinity with words and perhaps have a good imagination, it doesn't mean you can write. If it was that simple, editors, publishers and agents wouldn't reject so many submissions.

Not surprisingly, there are a vast number of books that offer guidance on writing – whether you want to write westerns, romantic fiction, articles, plays, screenplays, erotic fiction, thrillers, horror stories or science fiction, there'll be at least one book advising you how to go about it. And *Write a Western in 30 Days* is yet another!

The following list is a small selection of useful books on writing fiction:

Stein on Writing by Sol Stein (1995)

For 36 years Stein edited writers such as Jack Higgins, Budd Schulberg and James Baldwin. He understands characterisation, flashbacks and pace.

Fiction Writer's Handbook by Hallie & Whit Burnett (1975)

Preface by Norman Mailer. The Burnetts were co-editors of *Story Magazine* and published the first work of Salinger, Saroyan, Capote, McCullers. 'Inspiring, instructive and invaluable' – Erskine Caldwell.

On Writing by George V. Higgins (1990)

Humorous, sometimes bitchy overview of a number of authors, but always with points to make, such as quoting the best opening chapter he has ever read (from Hemingway's *A Farewell to Arms*).

On Writing: *A Memoir of the Craft* by Stephen King (2000)

Part memoir, part master class, and wholly fascinating.

The Writer's Journey by Christopher Vogler (1992)

One particularly helpful guide for potential writers is *The Writer's Journey* by Christopher Vogler. Subtitled *Mythic Structure for Storytellers and Screenwriters*, it has become one of the essential books to own if you take your writing seriously.

Vogler has evaluated over 6,000 screenplays for most of the big film studios. You may respond, 'I don't want to write a screenplay, I want to write a novel.' Every story you write, to some degree, should become a series of images in the reader's head. You have the chance to create pictures, emotions and dialogue in the reader's mind – if done well, the reader lives the fiction he or she is reading and vicariously travels in the story – essentially, a film of the mind.

Storytelling is ancient and respected. Most successful films and books seem to tap into a universal need. Influenced by Joseph Campbell's decades-old book *The Hero with a Thousand Faces*, Vogler began to work on a practical guide to storytelling.

Campbell stated that the most persistent theme in oral tradition and recorded literature was the myth of the hero. The thousand faces? A hero can be many things and face countless obstacles which change him – or her.

The myth of the hero falls into three acts – a format that harks back to Aristotle. In Act One the hero begins in the Ordinary World, then is Called to Adventure, but he Refuses, then he meets the Mentor and Crosses the first threshold. Act Two sees the hero beset by tests, befriended by allies and endangered by enemies, then he approaches the Inmost Cave and undergoes the Supreme Ordeal and is rewarded. Act Three sees the hero on the Road Back, his Resurrection or Change and his ultimate return with the Elixir.

But you don't want to write fantasy, you want to write a western? Fine; the hero's journey is all metaphor – symbols of universal life experiences. And all fiction is fantasy, isn't it? Anyway, worth a look.

Dictionary of First Names by Ernest Weekley (1939, reprinted 1994)

Contains over 3,000 first names used around the world, together with their derivations and meanings. Ideal source for historical fiction.

The Penguin Writer's Manual by Martin Manser and Stephen Curtis (2002)

Not only aimed at fiction writers, but it's an essential companion for anyone who wants to master the art of writing good English. Tells you all you need to know about grammar, usage, spelling and punctuation.

Usage and Abusage: A Guide to Good English by Eric Partridge, revised by Janet Whitcut (1942–1999)

The classic work looks at the use and constant misuse of English.

Merriam Webster's Manual for Writers & Editors (1999)

It's not a book about writing; it is a style guide, starting with punctuation, capitals, and abbreviations and culminating in typography, printing, and binding.

. *The Chicago Manual of Style 16th edition Online*

'Provides recommendations on editorial style and publishing practices for the digital age.' *$35 annual subscription*

Guides can't write the book for you, however

No, at risk of stating the obvious, you have to come up with the idea for the novel.

What research – and writing guides – do for you is, hopefully, inspire you so before long you're brimming with ideas!

4

Theme and ideas

The theme is the core of the novel. It can be simple, like good against bad, of course. Usually, it's much more complex than that, perhaps with more than one layer of theme.

It's quite possible that when you first devise your plot, you don't realize the themes running through the story. As the characters interact and the plot evolves, themes develop – jealousy, greed, and revenge, for example.

The story must say something about human life, even if in a historical context. It should reveal a plausible view of the human condition or problems of living in the Old West – 'a poetic truth', as Elizabeth Bowen called it. There has to be some human significance.

The theme shouldn't be too high-flown, naturally. It has to be coloured by the desired emotional effects you wish to evince.

You write to affect the reader, even if only to entertain; but usually you're also creating tension, anger, fear and perhaps tears – yes, even in a western.

Emotional response

Obviously, you can't predict how your readers will respond to your story and its theme, though there are enough eternal verities to fall back upon. The majority of readers will be affected by the problems encountered by your characters, providing you make them believable – that is the problems *and* the characters.

That's why you have to respect the genre. You'll begin to live your characters' lives and it is this connection with them that the reader latches on to, perhaps to the point where some empathy can be tapped.

Be true to your characters and your readers will usually

respond favourably.

Treat all of your characters as mere pawns in your plot and your readers won't engage with the story or your characters.

Taglines

The theme can be similar to the tagline of a film. Here are the main themes of some of my western novels. Underlying most of them, there are other themes too.

He came to town to find his lost love, but first he must kill her brother. *Death at Bethesda Falls*. Theme – revenge.

Chance threw her into his arms, but now he found himself gambling with the lives of a whole township. *Last Chance Saloon*. Theme – bravery.

They'd abducted his wife and blinded him, but that wasn't going to stop him finding her. *Blind Justice at Wedlock*. Theme – overriding love.

The past caught up with him in the form of his true love – and the man who betrayed him. *The $300 Man*. Theme – the past bites back.

They should be resting, retired, instead they had a showdown with young guns. *Old Guns*. Theme – age never wearies them.

As you will observe, certain themes predominate in a western. Revenge and bravery, for example. But you don't have to always opt for the most obvious. In my first western, *Death at Bethesda Falls*, I borrowed from English history – the misunderstanding between Henry II and Thomas á Beckett – to create murderous tension. Where Henry reportedly said, 'Who will rid me of this turbulent priest?' I had a villain ruing the influence of his schoolmarm sister... with the potential for similar tragic consequences.

Possible themes might be:

- Good versus evil
- Justice wins

- Right over might
- Pushing back the frontier
- Taming the land
- Taming a town
- Love conquers all
- Death isn't particular

... and so on...

Don't get stuck on finding a theme. If one doesn't spring to mind straight away, don't trouble yourself over it, just move on. It's probably already there and will present itself through your subconscious as you write.

Ideas

It's likely that you already have an idea or two that could make a western novel. Good. There's no shortage of material to inspire you and provide ideas and storylines.

Here, I'll simply jot down a brief overview of areas you might want to consider, should you need some guidance on subject matter to tackle. Needless to say, these ideas are not exhaustive.

- *Railroads.* Five days after the two ends of the railroad were joined at Promontory, paying passengers travelled on the transcontinental trains. Hitherto, a journey over the plains was a formidable undertaking, requiring time, energy and endurance. The six months' journey from Omaha, Nebraska to Sacramento was reduced to less than a week. The prairie schooner had virtually passed away. In 1870, the first full year of operation, nearly 150,000 passengers rode that line. Of course many passengers didn't make the full trip – they were short-haul travellers – cowhands, farmers, miners, hunters and Indians.
- There are plenty of stories about the railroaders building the permanent way, the mix of nations, the attacks by

Indians, the land-grabbing, the financiers, the shady deals and scandals.

○ There are the rail men and women involved in working the trains or supplying the food at the railroad stations, and of course the many cardsharps duping the unwary passengers.

○ Private rail cars were organised for 'safaris' for wealthy patrons on the Dakota prairies.

○ Picnics by rail became fashionable in California.

○ And of course there were the outlaws who robbed trains, destroying lives in the process.

○ Come the 1880s, immigrants from Russia and elsewhere in Europe rode the Northern Pacific to North Dakota, each with their story to tell.

○ Many more prosperous settlers even brought their own portable houses, trees and shrubs.

○ By 1893 there were five great rail systems spanning the West: the Atchison, Topeka & Santa Fe, the Great Northern, the Northern Pacific, the Southern Pacific and the Union Pacific. In *Old Guns*, my heroes board the Fremont, Elkhorn and Missouri Valley train for Deadwood.

• *Mining*. While prospectors had been in the West for years, the rush began in earnest in 1849 in California. From that point on, it seemed gold and silver miners were dubbed 'forty-niners'. Ten years later, another gold strike was made at Clear Creek by George Jackson near Colorado Springs. That same year the area around Denver was inundated with gold prospectors, due to announcements of small deposits being found in the South Platte River.

○ The majority of prospectors – there were up to 100,000 of them in that year alone – arrived ill-equipped and ignorant of the country and the hazards they faced. In the same year, the fabulous Comstock Lode was discovered in the Washoe Mountains of Nevada.

○ And notoriously, the 1876 gold strikes in the Black Hills spelled the doom of the Sioux. Mining doesn't just offer scope for relating the interaction of different conflicting miners, there's the panoply of settlers, camp followers, gamblers and villains that went along too – many seeking an easier way of making it rich than digging in the ground. Mining has its own jargon, such as sourdough, sluice, grubstake, but use it sparingly.

○ Notorious Deadwood sprang up in the Black Hills, where bankers were handling $100,000 a day.

○ Check out the fascinating characters – Henry Comstock, George Hearst and Adolph Sutro, for example.

○ The ore dug out of the earth generated wealth, townships, communities and greed – lots of greed.

○ Mining is featured in different ways in both *The $300 Man* and *Old Guns*.

• *Pioneers.* Settlers moved West in the 1840s using wagons of various types – Conestogas, prairie schooners, plains freighters – and continued until the coming of the railroads. So bear in mind that the backstory of some of your characters could involve their family moving West in the late 1840s and 1850s.

○ Settlement of the grasslands began about a decade before the Civil War, but only hesitantly.

○ Yet after the war, pioneers surged into the region by the tens of thousands – farmers from the Mississippi valley, disillusioned gold seekers from California and the Rockies, and of course wave after wave of immigrants from Europe.

○ When the well-timbered areas of Kansas, Nebraska and Minnesota had been occupied, newcomers spread further afield, further west into the prairies.

- ○ Homes would be simple affairs to begin with – some merely made from sod – but with time, patience and plenty of luck and pluck, their residences would grow and become sturdy and lasting homes.
- ○ And settlers also travelled up the Mississippi, using riverboats and paddle steamers, floating palaces with their fair share of gentlemen and villains.
- ○ Settlers had enough conflict in their lives, too – plagues of locusts, brush fires, the weather, the neighbours, the roaming Civil War vagrants, and speculators.

- *Townships*. Today, it's difficult perhaps to imagine, but towns of the Old West sprang up exceedingly fast, often beginning with several tents as temporary accommodation, until the wood could be delivered and the house built. In 1877, for example, within twelve days Garland City emerged from nothing to 105 houses and in another week that number was 200.

  - ○ A town of four months could boast of a population of about four hundred. Whole towns could be sold, thanks to the Township Act of 1844. A group of settlers or speculators could stake out 320 acres and take possession for the nominal sum of $125 an acre. The land was then divided into lots, which were sold to prospective townsmen. Profits could be huge, and of course chicanery was not unheard of, where a prospective townsman discovered later that he was the proud owner of a piece of paper 'not worth a damn'.
  - ○ By 1870, people could purchase by mail order a prefabricated house, though it might take a while to get the sections transported. And mail order brides were not unusual, either...
  - ○ Remember that communities would be ravaged by cholera, typhoid, diphtheria, pneumonia, pleurisy and smallpox. The weak, the old and the infants bore the

brunt of illnesses; the wagon trains' trails were grim testimony to the grief, with crosses erected in their wake. It's the surviving mother and children who might provide profound storylines.

○ Spiritual guidance was plentiful. On the grasslands, the Methodists were usually first on the scene, closely followed by Presbyterians, Congregationalists, Baptists and Roman Catholics, each with their own conflicting view of God.

○ There's scope for a story or ten about town promoters, selling land and promises, during the period 1850–1880.

○ A western town is rich in material – meat market, real estate and loan agent, advocate office, drug store, dry goods and clothing, general store, dress making, fruits, beer parlour, restaurant, schoolhouse, jail and church, to name a few establishments, all with their tales to tell.

○ Naturally, there was entertainment, too – from the unsavoury to the family-oriented; all tastes catered for, it seemed. *HMS Pinafore* was performed in Topeka, Kansas in 1888, so don't neglect concert hall acts of the period, or famous thespians, such as Lola Montez, mistress to King Ludwig of Bavaria (she appears in George MacDonald Fraser's Flashman novel, *Royal Flash*); and Sarah Bernhardt, who appeared in *Camille* at the opera house in St Joseph, Missouri in 1881. And famous authors gave readings in saloons and more salubrious establishments, among them Oscar Wilde as can be seen in *Wilde West* (1991) and Charles Dickens.

• *Ranchers*. These were men and women who found a land that brought out the best in them, and they had to be resolute to survive. They had to cope with solitude, failure, unremitting hard work and the added hazards of grappling with nature and with each other.

- The heyday of Western ranching was from 1866 to 1886, during which time ranchers shipped more than ten million head of cattle and one million sheep to markets in the East. They employed 40,000 cowboys and herders over that time.
- In the early days, land was cheap or even free for the taking. They had to defend what they took, however, against Indians, rustlers, squatters and other ranchers.
- At the end of the Civil War, Confederate Texas was suffering from a glut of cattle, their breeding unabated during the conflict. With the cowboys off fighting, the cattle were unbranded. Ranchers couldn't afford to keep so many head: 'A man's poverty was estimated by the number of cattle he possessed'. Thus began the cattle trails to hungry northerners, as exemplified by the Pulitzer prize-winning *Lonesome Dove* (1985) by Larry McMurtry.
- Plenty of outlaws got rich by herding the unbranded cattle; others resorted to rustling from the cattle drives. Mexican Juan Cortina, heading one of the biggest bands, excused his thievery by saying it was revenge against the hated Texans, and thus many of his men descended into murderous bloodletting.
- In 1860, the Texas Rangers were disbanded but were re-established to combat the plague of rustling, and they were hugely successful.
- By an act of Congress reservation Indians were each allotted 730 pounds of beef a year, attracting many ranchers to vie for beef contracts. And of course there's the conflict between cattlemen and sheepmen. While it took seven mounted cowboys to move a 1,000 head of cattle, a single herder on foot with a good dog could tend the same number of sheep. Perhaps the most distinctive sheepherders were the Basques, from the

Pyrenees.

- ○ The first practical barbed wire came on the scene in 1874, so don't think of using it in a novel set earlier.
- ○ Not all ranchers owned immense spreads; some had small herds and a tough hardscrabble life to contend with, every member of the family mucking in.

- *Soldiers*. The Indian Wars are part of the Old West story. The wars don't have to be central to your tale, but they could serve as a backdrop or as a relevant backstory. A little research on the frontier army of the time will supply more than enough material.

  - ○ A soldier would be tough, surviving hardship, attack, starvation, thirst and perhaps even wounding.
  - ○ There's a tendency for western heroes to be ex-Cavalry or ex-Civil War soldiers. That's fine – just ensure that your research makes him believable.
  - ○ Oddly, black cowboys and soldiers – the latter named 'buffalo soldiers' by the Indians – haven't figured much in genre westerns a great deal, yet there were hundreds of freedmen who took to cowboying and soldiering with verve and distinction. Frank Roderus' *The Outsider* (1988) and Brian Garfield's *Tripwire* (1973) are honourable exceptions; there are others, but not too many. Latterly, there seem to be more books about ex-buffalo soldiers appearing.
  - ○ Remember also that some officers and enlisted men had their wives with them in their frontier forts – the wives lifted morale and perhaps caused the occasional scandal. There would be jealousies and illicit liaisons, perhaps an officer's wife attracted to a trooper.
  - ○ Beginning in 1881, the sale of liquor was prohibited in forts. This resulted in the blossoming of several off-post saloons, known as hog ranches, where they supplied a steady stream of whiskey, beer and prostitutes.

- Wives of enlisted men and non-coms often served as laundresses in the fort's Suds Row, and occasionally as midwives or nurses.
- Many a soldier was denied permission to get married, since the number of married enlisted men in a regiment was governed by the need for laundresses; Army regulations imposed a quota of one laundress to every nineteen and a half men.
- Any eligible female who arrived on the post was courted by hordes of lonely soldiers. This meant that officers' maids got married, so often the officer's wife would enlist an Eastern employment agency to send out only homely unlovely girls. It made no difference; even these young women were married within two months of their arrival on post. Officers therefore hired soldiers as servants for their families; they were called strikers and earned additional pay. The practice was made illegal in 1870 but went on regardless.
- As you can see, there's scope for several good storylines based at a frontier post.

- *Women.* As has already been mentioned, the West was full of promise for women. That promise was often unfettered freedom, something they couldn't have enjoyed within the constraints of 'polite society' in the East or Europe.
  - Naturally, she had to fight off Indian raids, endure starvation, privation and even a terrible sense of being alone in a seemingly endless, empty land.
  - But she had power, too – to press for new schools, churches, law and order, improved morality.
  - An inducement to marriage was the Donation Land Act of 1850 in Oregon Territory: a husband and wife were entitled to twice the acreage that a single man could claim. And of course a wife meant an extra pair of hands to do the work, with doubtless more 'willing' hands

available in due course from their children. Maybe not so much freedom there, then...

○ The Homestead Act of 1862 enticed single women as well as men West with equal opportunity to become landowners. Five years of toil could earn a deed for several acres of land.

○ By 1900 women had won the vote in four Western states.

○ Keeping in touch with family back East relied on the mail – which could take as much as six months for a letter to reach its destination; that is, before the coming of the railroad. Poor communication is a useful tool for characters in a story.

○ Pregnant wives had to work virtually till the baby was due – hard, gruelling work, too. One wife wrote that the week before giving birth she cooked for fifteen men brought in to work on the farm, and then she'd collapse on her bed, tired out.

○ Drink, drugs and family violence – some of the crosses a wife has to bear. Times don't change, perhaps because people don't.

○ Some books have been written about white women captured by Indians and then being returned to their own people and ostracised, such as *The Pride of Hannah Wade* (1985); yet there's still mileage in that storyline.

○ And there's scope for revisionist views on women in the West, bringing with them education, decency and even literature and art.

• *Civil War*. The great national tragedy that Lincoln's Secretary of State once called the 'irrepressible conflict' isn't technically part of the Old West. But 'the War Between the States' had countless repercussions in the Old West. Indeed, 'the late unpleasantness' still causes ripples if not waves in the present day.

- *Confederate states.* These were Texas, Arkansas, Louisiana, Mississippi, Tennessee, Georgia, Florida, South Carolina and Virginia. So if your characters – or their families – came from one of these states, their lives would be affected greatly, since after the war these states suffered great privation.

- In the early days, the Union organised blockades of the southern states. So, Confederate blockade runners sprang up – lean, swift, ghostly vessels, bringing much-needed weaponry, ammunition, goods and food. Naturally, such commerce generated wealth in certain quarters – and enmity in others.

- Inevitably, as in so many civil wars, families were torn apart. Some family members wanted to stay loyal to the United States, while others wished to go their own way outside the Union. Jefferson Davis said, afterwards, 'The hope of our people was to escape from injury and strife in the Union, to find prosperity and peace out of it.'

- *Beginning of the conflict.* Threat of war brewed for almost thirty years but became a reality on 12 April, 1861, when the conflict started with the Charleston bombardment of Fort Sumter, a Union-fort built on a shoal in Charleston harbour. Confederate Brig. Gen Beauregard's guns poured more than 3,000 shells into the fort. The fort's commander, Major Robert Anderson surrendered and all of his garrison were allowed to march away free, with flags flying, and headed for New York.

- There are legends of stolen and lost gold shipments – so many, you could probably trip over a cache every day on your way round the battlegrounds. Grist to the writer's mill.

- Atrocities were committed on both sides, against

civilians as well as opposing soldiers, and these have been used in revenge themed novels.

○ There are dozens of battles and skirmishes, all well documented, any of which could be used for a flashback. I used the battle of Fort Fisher, at the close of the conflict, in *The $300 Man*.

There's a rich seam of storytelling gold in the countless books on the period and the above selection barely scratches the surface.

5

Point of view decision

As you'd expect, character point of view (POV) is a very important subject for writers of any genre fiction. I'm specifying genre fiction here: literary fiction gets away with switching POV at the drop of a thought. I'll come to POV switching shortly.

First, you need to decide on the POV you're going to adopt for your western.

What are the options?

- First Person
  The character narrates everything as he sees it. This is the most intimate POV, because the reader is always in the narrator's head. The classic version is perhaps *True Grit* (1968) by Charles Portis, reminiscences of Mattie, an elderly woman, thinking back to when she was a fourteen-year-old in the West.

  Not many westerns are written using this POV, and the reasons for this are many and varied. The action is limited to what the narrator sees and hears. The narrator has to be privy to everything – or learns second-hand by reported speech. The main character, the narrator, is never in serious jeopardy, since he or she survives to tell us the tale. So the writer must place in danger other characters close to the narrator, in order to crank up suspense and concern.

  Here is a sample, from the beginning of a western. Classic start – the main character is riding into town.

  I eased the sorrel horse to a halt on the outskirts of the small town of Benson Butte, which nestled at the base of the mountain's foothills. Briefly, I removed my flat-crowned black hat and beat it against my pants legs and shirt, and cast off trail dust, revealing black clothes. For some time now, I always wore black. Black because I was in mourning. Mourning the men I'd killed.

I used a silk neckerchief to wipe the sweat from my brow. Sitting here, travel-weary, I felt a lot older than twenty-six.

The signboard at the side of the road announced:

WELCOME TO

BENSON BUTTE

FOUNDED 1856

POP. ~~502.~~ 501

If my last informant was square, then I'd be giving whoever painted that sign the job of reducing the population count by yet one more.

No great loss to the world, I reckoned, gently urging the sorrel towards the livery stable at the end of the main street, over on the right.

Like so many similar small towns in Dakota Territory, Benson Butte comprised a long main street with a small cluster of buildings that formed short side streets that spread east and west. There was a strong hint of more expansion on the east side, with two new buildings half-completed; so, even after only ten years of life, the town was clearly flourishing. At the north end, tinted a rose glow from the dying sun, loomed Garfield Mountain, while to my left were cultivated fields that sloped down towards Clarence Creek and several smaller water courses. A pleasant place for a killing.

I reined in at Zeke's Livery and slowly swung a leg over the saddlebags and tarp-covered bedroll and stepped down. I almost sensed the ache ease out of my bones as I felt the firm ground underfoot. The bullwhip tied to my belt knocked gently against my thigh, reminding me of the last man I'd whipped during a question-and-answer session. I got my answers. I adjusted my weapons belt, tied down the two holsters, and then looped the reins over the hitching rail.

Here, we don't know the narrator's name. That will come when he introduces himself to someone, maybe the livery stable man. We don't know what he looks like – that will have to come when he studies himself in a mirror, maybe while shaving or checking for damage after a fight.

Everything has to be seen through the narrator's eyes.

- Second Person

  Second person narrative has its advocates, but it generally smacks of a literary device and doesn't make easy reading, particularly when at novel length or in genre fiction. Here, the writer is speaking directly to the reader, even addressing him as 'you', as if he existed in the narrator's world.

  You have to go along the ledge; but you can't. Your body, tremulous with fear, is too self-serving to move.

  The vast majority of beginners should avoid this POV.

- Third Person Single

  Here, we follow the main character throughout, and we see the world through his or her eyes, and read his thoughts, and again several of the constraints of the first person POV are still evident. The character is in every scene and reacts accordingly. Any danger that presents itself is perhaps more heightened, because he or she can die at the end.

  It's the same as the next POV, save that it never deviates from one character to another.

- Third Person Multiple

  This is the most popular POV stance for genre fiction, and especially westerns. Now, the writer can show people and thoughts in scenes not shared by the main character.

If someone is arranging an ambush, then the reader can be aware of it while the main character isn't. Suspense has been introduced by this simple expedient.

Different scenes can be seen from different characters' viewpoints. So we can read the thoughts of someone other than the main character.

Many beginners fall into the trap of showing the thoughts of several characters within the same scene. While this is feasible – and is done in the next POV type – it isn't recommended, as it can quickly lead to reader confusion. Another problem with head-jumping, as it's called, is that the connection the reader has with the scene's character is jolted at each switch, so the narrative flow suffers.

Here is the same sample text, but instead of being narrated by 'I', it's by 'he'.

He eased his sorrel horse to a halt on the outskirts of the small town of Benson Butte, which nestled at the base of the mountain's foothills. Briefly, he removed his flat-crowned black hat and beat it against his pants legs and shirt, and cast off trail dust, revealing black clothes. For some time now, he'd taken to wearing only black. Black because he was in mourning. Mourning the men he'd killed.

He rested the hand that held the reins on the pommel and with his free hand used his silk neckerchief to wipe the sweat from his brow. Sitting here, travel-weary, he felt a lot older than twenty-six.

The signboard at the side of the road announced:
WELCOME TO
BENSON BUTTE
FOUNDED 1856
POP. ~~502.~~ 501
If his last informant was square, then he would be giving

whoever painted that sign the job of reducing the population count by yet one more.

No great loss to the world, he opined, gently urging the sorrel towards the livery stable at the end of the main street, over on the right.

Like so many similar small towns in Dakota Territory, Benson Butte comprised a long main street with a small cluster of buildings forming short side streets that spread east and west. There was a strong hint of more expansion on the east side, with two new buildings half-completed; so, even after only ten years of life, the town was clearly flourishing. At the north end, tinted a rose glow from the dying sun, loomed Garfield Mountain, while to his left were cultivated fields sloping down towards Clarence Creek and several smaller water courses.

He reined in at Zeke's Livery and slowly swung his leg over his saddlebags and tarp-covered bedroll and stepped down. He almost sensed the ache ease out of his bones as he felt the firm ground under his hand-tooled boots. The bullwhip tied to his belt knocked gently against his thigh, reminding him of the last man he'd whipped during a question-and-answer session. He got his answers. He adjusted his weapons belt, tied down the two holsters, and then looped the reins over the hitching rail.

Again, we don't know the man's name, because it's his viewpoint. In our internal world, we don't think about our name, just about what we see and feel. The name and description will have to come later, in conversation perhaps.

However, as this is multiple third person, at this juncture in the story we could switch to a bystander's POV and watch the man ride into town, observe the black clothes, the weather-beaten features, the grey eyes etc.

- Omniscient

This POV could also be termed 'omnipotent' since the writer is behaving almost in a godlike manner, all-powerful where his creations are concerned.

Omniscient POV lets the reader see all and hear all, and often from a point hovering somewhere just above the scene – indeed, as if the reader was a film director, rather than an actor in the story. Descriptions of the scenery no longer have to be formed from the mind of a single character; it can be narrated by the author. Naturally, more writerly turns of phrase can be employed – which wouldn't be recommended when viewed from a character's perspective.

However, the downside with the omniscient POV is that the reader cannot engage with any one character – they're all flooding the reader's mind at some point. So the reader is at least one place removed from the troubles and travails of the characters. It's a story, and can be seen as such. Whereas with first person or third person, the reader can become lost in the world of the primary character, and vicariously share all the feelings and fears and hopes.

So-called literary fiction, when done well, can employ the omniscient POV and also make you feel for the variety of characters – *Lonesome Dove*, for example. In that book, there's a lot of head-jumping yet we still get captivated by Gus McCrae.

• Mix and match

Some modern thrillers alternate between first person narrative and third person multiple. Surprisingly, despite forcing the reader to jump out of the story at each switch, this can work – in the hands of an accomplished writer, such as Harlan Coben. I wouldn't recommend it for westerns – but it's still an option.

Westerns mix omniscient and usually third person to some extent. The classic instance is at the beginning, when the loner rides into town. We're seeing him perhaps from a crane shot, studying his clothes, his weapons, his features, homing in on him. And then the switch is made – we enter his thoughts and learn why he is riding into town.

For this final example, essentially using the same beginning, I've opted for the combined omniscient and third person. Most of the novel will be in multiple third person, but it's helpful to the reader at times to step back and show a broader picture (omniscient).

Jake Storm eased his sorrel horse to a halt on the outskirts of the small town of Benson Butte, which nestled at the base of the mountain's foothills. He was dressed entirely in black. Black because he was in mourning. Mourning the men he had killed.

Every movement that he made in the saddle was slow and considered. He rested the hand that held the reins on the pommel and with his free hand nudged the flat brim, pushing the flat-crowned hat to the back of his head. He used his silk neckerchief to wipe the sweat from his tanned and lined brow; his weathered features suggested that he was a lot older than his twenty-six years.

The signboard at the side of the road announced:
WELCOME TO
BENSON BUTTE
FOUNDED 1856
POP. ~~502.~~ 501

If his last informant was square, then he would be giving whoever painted that sign the job of reducing the population count by yet one more.

No great loss to the world, he opined, gently urging the sorrel towards the livery stable at the end of the main street, over on the right.

Like so many similar small towns that were springing up in Dakota Territory, Benson Butte comprised a long main street with a small cluster of buildings forming short side streets that spread east and west. There was a strong hint of more expansion on the east side, with two new buildings half-completed; so, even after only ten years of life, the town was clearly flourishing. At the north end, tinted a rose glow from the dying sun, loomed Garfield Mountain, while to Storm's left were cultivated fields sloping down towards Clarence Creek and several smaller water courses.

Storm reined in at Zeke's Livery and slowly swung his leg over his saddlebags and tarp-covered bedroll and stepped down.

He almost sensed the ache ease out of his bones as he felt the firm ground under his hand-tooled boots. The bullwhip tied to his belt knocked gently against his thigh, reminding him of the last man he'd whipped during a question-and-answer session. He got his answers.

He adjusted his weapons belt, tied down the two holsters, and then looped the reins over the hitching rail.

This combined version lets the writer have the best of both worlds, as long as the switch between omniscient and third person isn't done too often to become distracting.

At once, the rider can be identified.

We can watch, as if from above, every movement he makes. We can note his appearance, his complexion and delve into his thoughts. We can use his name – though sparingly.

In the next scene, we could enter the head of the hostler in the livery, as well as staying with Storm too. I'd advise against it, but with the omniscient POV you can do that.

Only slip into another character's POV if the switch is worthwhile – does it tell the reader something that can't be gleaned by staying in the same POV?

Whatever POV you adopt, it should be consistent, so

that you don't push your reader out of the story, confuse and confound or even lose your reader entirely.

Changing POV

If you change a character POV in a scene, then create a scene break. I won't labour the point, but an example can be found on p. 79 of *The $300 Man*.

Corbin too wondered what business Tillman had with Mr Walker.

Sitting in an upholstered chair opposite Mr Walker who was at his desk, Tillman rested his elbows on the arms and nursed a tumbler of bourbon and branch water. 'I am perplexed, Mr Walker.'

Thanks to the break, the reader then knows whose head he or she is in – Corbin's then Tillman's.

Action

Action scenes can be difficult where there's a temptation to show how each fighter feels as the blows are exchanged. Resist this. In fact, for each scene, decide whose POV is going to be revealed.

When the scene is first written, I'm not always sure whose POV I'm going to write from, as I'm just writing the interplay, the dialogue and the action. But when I have to layer in the emotion – and possibly thoughts and feelings, such as pain – then I have to decide. Who is most affected in the scene? Then that's probably whose POV you should use – so go back through that scene and personalize it from that character's perspective.

Bert laughed and tugged off the woman's wedding band. She whimpered but said nothing.

Elijah chuckled. 'Get another husband, widow. He'll buy a

new ring for you!'

These distractions were enough. Half rising, Corbin swung his left arm up, the hook sinking into Elijah's neck. Blood spurted, splashing Corbin's dark blue flannel shirt and buckskin jacket. Damn, must have hit an artery. Jerking his bloody hook out of the wound, he used it to snag the shotgun out of Elijah's hands.

Bert swerved round, levelling his six-gun, his face draining white at sight of his sibling crumpling to the carriage floor.

Corbin's right hand grabbed the shotgun. Resting the barrel on the back of the seat, he blasted Bert full in the chest before the bandit could fire off a single bullet.

The widow shrieked in alarm as Bert fell back on to the floor, ineffectually gripping his revolver. Others cheered. (*The $300 Man*, pp. 7/8)

In the above example, there are four characters – Bert and Elijah, the bad guys, the widow and Corbin. It would be easy to get into any or all of their heads – but this must be resisted. This has to be from Corbin Molina's POV throughout. 'These distractions were enough' is Corbin's thought. I don't convey it as 'he thought' when it's obvious by the next three words that it's Corbin's POV. Then Corbin's thought – Damn... It's visual and fast, and we don't get confused about who's doing what.

Mixed up action

Action scenes can easily become confusing, especially where the writer is employing 'he' but it isn't always obvious who 'he' is. There's a tendency to jump from one character POV to another. Pay close attention to your action scenes, and make sure you've pinned down whose POV you're writing.

Strive to simplify and visualise every time.

Cheat on occasion

1) First section in Chapter 3 is from Corbin Molina's POV. However,

> Together, the hobo Jeremiah and Corbin Molina stepped out into the morning sun and headed for the café on the other side of the wide street.
>
> Sheriff Deshler took off his hat and scratched the back of his head. 'That Jeremiah doesn't know how close he came to knocking on the gates of hell.' (p. 45)

You'll notice that Corbin has left, so he can't see or hear the Sheriff. That's a cheat.

2) Last section in Chapter 3 is from Sheriff Deshler's POV. However,

> Stella giggled. 'Maybe we'll rob it as well.' Suddenly she clubbed Deshler on the head with the rifle butt. 'That's so he gets no ideas about chasing after us.' (p. 51)
>
> You'll note that Deshler was knocked unconscious, so he couldn't hear her last words. That's a cheat. In these cheats, it's as if we're playing at movie director.

Food

This subject has been mentioned already, in the research chapter. It's worth reiterating, however. If a POV character has a meal, then the reader should see what he or she is eating. 'He ate his meal' is just 'tell' and isn't good enough. 'Show' – and you show by giving at the very least a brief description of the food. No need to over-egg it – no pun intended.

On p. 132 of *The $300 Man*, for example:

> Corbin thought that Dr Malinda Dix looked every inch the Southern lady with her flounced skirt trimmed with ruches. Taking his eyes off her for a moment, he cut the layers of

tender deer meat and eggplant and used the dining fork attached to his metal stump; the crushed green tomatoes and Parmesan cheese added to the taste as he chewed.

So I show Corbin eating deer meat and eggplant, crushed green tomatoes and Parmesan cheese. Earlier, on p. 84:

Stomach full with Chili de Sangre Anaranjada, Corbin read the local newspaper in the hotel lounge, allowing the beef and pork to digest. He had complimented the chef, a Swede by the moniker of Iwan Morelius. Apparently, Morelius had been on the staff of Baron Ernst Mattias Peter von Vegesack, who had been given leave to fight for the Union. While the baron returned to Sweden after the war, Morelius stayed and Mr Canaan, the hotel manager, was vociferously proud of his culinary acquisition.

In my writing workshops, I'm constantly saying, 'Don't neglect the food!' Research the period, obviously, and add taste as well as looks to the culinary offering.

Books

I have a similar gripe with authors who mention that a character is 'reading a good book' but we, the readers, have no idea what the book is called.

If the character is reading a book, then we should *see* the title, since we're viewing it through the character's eyes. A little research should come up with an appropriate title for the period.

6

Book and chapter titles

The title of your book should attract the reader's attention and even provide sufficient intrigue so that the cover will be turned over and the first page will be read. If the cover and title do that, it's done the job. Of course, it helps if the title is memorable!

The title should be one or all of these:

- Phrased concisely
- Expressed in concrete terms – not abstract ones
- Able to arouse curiosity concerning the main character's predicament
- Fresh

Often, the ideal method to conjure up a suitable title is to fasten on an aspect of the book's conflict.

A turn of phrase that sums up the underlying theme might work, too.

Or play on the words: *Blind Justice at Wedlock* was about the hero being blinded and seeking justice. I couldn't simply use *Blind Justice*, as that title was already overused. There is no copyright for a book title, but it pays to check that your title hasn't just been released into the marketplace. If it was used several years ago, then that's not a big problem, but if the title is recent, then it can cause confusion. It might also suggest that it's not particularly original.

Sometimes, a phrase from a quotation might serve. Beware of using quotations from individuals who have not been dead for at least seventy years – they're probably still in copyright and you might need to get permission to use the quotation. Prolific author E.V. Thompson's story about early Texas, *Cry Once Alone* (1984) used this title from a lengthy quotation of Comanche Chief Ten Bears.

Generally, one-word titles rarely work in the memorability stakes. If there hadn't been a film featuring Paul Newman, would the book *Hombre* be memorable? Probably not. One-word titles don't evoke any image in the mind's eye, particularly if they're abstract – hence, the recommendation to use concrete terms.

Yet, to contradict that observation, they've always been popular with western writers – not least, Louis L'Amour: *Brionne, Callaghen, Catlow, Chancy, Conagher, Fallon, Flint, Hondo, Matagorda, Shalako, Sitka*, and *Sackett*, among others, so perhaps it's the exception that proves the rule? If the title is a character's name or the town's name, it might work.

In the end, maybe it comes down to personal preference. But don't always go for the simplest option – the character's or the town's name.

Sometimes, the theme is significant and can be used for the title, as long as it isn't too abstract.

Indeed, the title might depend on whether or not you've decided to write about a series character. That may dictate a slightly different approach to selecting a title. Oliver Strange's character Sudden, for example, started out with the book *The Range Robbers* (1930) but was followed by *Sudden* (1933) and six more with the Sudden name in the title.

Certain words tend to crop up in western novel titles. Some clichéd, others not. Words such as:

- guns,
- death,
- showdown,
- trail,
- hills,
- rifle,
- creek,

- falls,
- butte,
- valley,
- canyon,
- brand, to name but a few.

You'll get a flavour from Appendix E, a small list of western fiction.

Don't get bogged down thinking about a title. Quite a number of authors simply use a 'working title' just to get started, feeling sure that by the time the book's finished, a title will come to mind.

Chapter headings

There's no requirement to label your chapters. Simply use plain numbers or Chapter 1, 2, 3 etc., or variations.

However, I like to use titles, and often play with words. My first western's Chapter One was entitled *Rue the Lash* – which was a play on the old western film star Lash LaRue. Sad, I know, but maybe a few old hands made the connection. Anyway, a whip did figure in the chapter.

You don't have to have a Prologue; and even if you do have one, you don't have to have an Epilogue. Some writers – and readers! – don't bother with prologues. I try to use the Prologue and Epilogue to bookend the tale; in my latest, *Old Guns*, the Prologue is *Penitentiary*, the place where the story begins; and the Epilogue is called *Penitent*, and it ends in the penitentiary. The hook in *The $300 Man* has already been explained.

And in that latter book, Chapter One's title, *Heaven's Gateway*, is the name of a bordello. An apt name, from the male perspective, I imagine. Other titles – *Behind every good man* – a phrase I revised to 'you'll find a bad woman'. *Lean Pickings* – I was tempted to call it Slim Pickings, another play on words, but desisted in deference to the western actor, Slim Pickens. And *The*

Pen is Mightier doesn't need elaboration – and it proved thus, since Corbin stabbed a villain in his eye with a pen.

Don't fret over chapter headings, either. Use them if you're inclined – but it's best to wait till the book is finished and after you've decided how to break up the western into chapters.

Certainly, you don't have to plan what happens in each chapter – just let the story flow. But you do need to have a map to your destination, even if it's a bit rough around the edges.

That map is the plot-plan.

7

Plot-plan

The plot thickens

Plot is the story's engine, drawing various events together and relating the consequences of characters' actions in response to those events. Plot tells you about *cause and effect*.

Some stories are character-driven while the plot drives others. It depends on the type of story. An action-adventure tale will move at a swift pace through several twisting and turning subplots while a love story may linger on the dilemmas faced by a number of star-crossed characters. Needless to say, both of these story types fall within the remit of westerns. Whatever type of story it is, both character and plot must be in harmony.

A plot-heavy story will seem contrived and keep the reader at a distance. Also, the plot will appear as the major character and the reader can't root for a plot. On the other hand, a character-rich tale will pull the reader in to the point where the plot is not evident but simply obstacles faced by this character you've grown to know. So, character tends to win over plot – but there still needs to be a plot to threaten the protagonist's world, livelihood or life.

Plots are relatively easy to think up, it seems. They must be. More than once I've been accosted by a would-be writer saying, 'I've got this great plot for a novel. Will you write it for me?' Well, no, thanks, I've got more than enough of my own to work on.

I don't recommend that you emulate Henry James, either. He said, 'When I sit down to write a novel I do not at all know, and I do not very much care, how it is to end.'

Some writers don't have a plot when they start – whether it's a short story or a novel. They have the kernel of an idea, or a theme, or even an ending in mind. Then they throw in a few characters and see how they react to their situation. It works for some. Tolkien was well into *The Fellowship of the Ring* when he put his hobbits inside an inn and introduced a ruffian called Strider. At that point Tolkien didn't know who Strider was or where the book was going!

Others plan each scene in fine detail, leaving nothing to chance and revel in the constraint this imposes.

Most writers probably fall somewhere in between these two extremes. It depends on the material and that initial spark. If a particular character leaps out at the writer, wanting to be written about, then it invariably becomes a character-driven tale. Private detective Maisie Dobbs jumped fully formed into Jacqueline Winspear's mind while she stopped her car at traffic lights! If a clever twist on a standard theme has popped into the mind, then the test is how to lead up to that twist ending.

Raymond Chandler wasn't particularly good at plotting. Often, he'd come to a point in his book, buried in a mess of conflicting plot-lines, when he wouldn't have a clue whodunit. During the filming of *The Big Sleep*, which has a convoluted plot, Howard Hawks wired Chandler to find out who killed the chauffeur. Chandler wired back: *I don't know!*

Writing a novel is much easier if you have a plot to follow. It doesn't mean you're in a rut. The plot is a rough-and-ready road. As the story progresses, you'll find that characters will want to take the occasional more interesting byway. Some writers let the characters wander off at a tangent and never rejoin the original plotted road; others are hard taskmasters and bring the character back in line after a fascinating diversion.

Plots should stem from the motivation of your characters. So it's vital that you get to know the people in your story.

Invariably, you will also be writing to a theme in your story. Make sure that this central idea runs through the novel and is embodied in one or more characters' thoughts and actions.

A plot without conflict is not much of a plot. Suffice to say that drama must contain some obstacle the protagonist has to overcome.

By carefully preparing your plot beforehand, you control the occasional diversions and bring everything back on track. By getting to know your characters before starting, you have a good idea how they will react to your plot and how they will shape the story.

Nothing is cast in stone. On occasion I have found that the initial plot was too simplistic and the characters, as they became fleshed out in the writing, suggested more logical and stronger plot directions to take. That's fine, as long as you remain in charge and don't let the story completely unravel.

Good plots need to be consistent, convincing and contain character interaction. Weak plots simply take the reader from point A to point B and are usually implausible – they haven't been thought through.

A story is often about a character's growth or change through adversity, which is brought about by facing obstacles and overcoming them. Though sometimes unwelcome, change is inevitable in life; in fiction, change is vitally necessary. The plot provides the means for the character to evolve.

For your novel, it's necessary to introduce subplots, which can be tests for secondary characters as well as the main protagonist. Yet these subplots must move the story forward, serve a purpose and reinforce the theme.

Convoluted plots exist, but they often appear contrived and lose all but the most attentive reader, so it's advisable to steer clear of complex plot structures in your western.

Every writer enters into a contract with the reader. The writer should not cheat. If the plot requires a twist, then that should be hinted at earlier rather than just being tagged on at the end.

The basic plot unit
This consists of a conflict test followed by a distinct emotional

response. In the response you show how the main character comes out of the test.

Naturally, for your western novel, you stack several plot units on top of each other, twisting the screw for the main character at every turn.

Drama is built by the introduction of new obstacles, thus delaying and intensifying the final conclusion. The most serious conflict test should be reserved for the end.

The final plot unit

The Black Moment. The main character seems overwhelmed by his difficulties, obstacles etc.; it's the moment when he seems forced to abandon his purpose – or life itself. When this final obstacle confronts him, all his previous emotional crises pale into insignificance.

The black moment can be conveyed as deep emotional despair, where the hero perceives no way out. This is seen time and again in suspense and action films – the hero or heroine overcomes obstacle after obstacle, but then there's the greatest yet to be faced, something that seems insurmountable and even soul-destroying. That's when the protagonist has to delve deep into his character to rise above this final terrible adversity.

The stages of plotting in a story

- Desired emotion. Decide which emotion you want to arouse in the reader
- Theme. Choose a theme – a statement with a verb in it – that is in tune with the emotion you want to produce.
- Main character's emotional drive. Choose a principal character whose major emotional trait is essential to the theme and the desired emotional effect.
- Main character's purpose. Give the protagonist a specific purpose – one clearly arising from his major emotional trait; it must be of the utmost importance to him and must

fit the theme.

- Conflict tests. Note all the possible obstacles to the protagonist's purpose.

- Initial clash. Begin setting up the obstacles to force the protagonist to choose between two or more alternative courses of action. The emphasis is on action here. Westerns are books about action.

- Dramatic high spot and the protagonist's emotional trait in active response. Again, there has to be an *active* response on the part of your main character. We don't want passive, here, in an action novel. And we don't want the hero being saved by others. Demonstrate his or her major emotional trait in the way they struggle to overcome the opposition.

- Additional conflict tests, high spots and the main character's active responses. Introduce subsequent conflict tests and again demonstrate the protagonist using his major emotional drive to overcome them.

- Final conflict and result. Define the Black Moment, the final conflict crisis and lastly demonstrate how the protagonist resolves the situation, possibly at great personal cost.

Not every author uses a plan when they come to plot a novel, as already mentioned. Some authors start to write and then see where the story and the characters lead them. I wouldn't recommend this, because the problem with that approach is that you could end up writing several chapters and many thousands of words, only to find that you've written yourself into a corner or haven't got enough storyline to sustain a full-length book.

There's no right or wrong way to approach the writing of a novel, only preferred ways.

However, if you're serious about writing a western in 30 days, I must reiterate that creating a plan is the only sensible route to take.

By now you'll have decided on a theme, maybe even a title,

and character POV. The prompt for the story or theme may come from a character who has popped into your head or who lived in the Old West and inspired the storyline. Whatever the source of the story, you now need to set down a rough outline – the plot-plan.

This can be a detailed blow-by-blow storyline or it can be sketches of various scenes spaced throughout the story. Some authors envisage major scenes and then link them up into a full novel.

There are no straight answers. I find that it can be a mixture of both – plot and character. To a large extent, it depends on your original impetus – that germ that's grown into the idea for a western novel.

My first western book began with a phrase I'd thought of many years before: *He wore only black. Black because he was in mourning. Mourning the men he'd killed.*

But then I had to explain it and expand it. That meant I had to examine the main character and his motivation. Asking why he was intent on seeking out a certain man. I decided to complicate matters for the hero, so the man he wanted to kill was the brother of the woman our hero loved. And it was while building his character that I also went on to develop the other interacting people – the brother and the woman he wanted to marry, for example. When their backstories were fleshed out, they provided additional plot and subplot.

The plot-plan isn't going to come fully formed. It will evolve. Begin with the bare bones, the time and place, the main characters – limit these to begin with; others will be introduced – or even introduce themselves – as the plot and story develops.

Your plot-plan should introduce the main characters early on, and their motivation should be illustrated.

Introduce conflict as soon as possible – it's conflict that holds the reader's attention. Of course, the conflict doesn't have to be physical in form, it can be emotional or threatening to livelihood or home or even provided by natural elements. Not always, but some form of quest is central to the protagonist.

In the following plot-plan illustration, it's the hero's duty to seek out bank robbers, no matter what the personal cost. A strong love interest is most certainly not out of place in a western – and allows for powerful emotional conflict.

As in the classic Aristotelian three-act play, your story needs to have its ups and downs, where your protagonist overcomes problems only to be faced with greater obstacles, until the resolution at the climax of the tale.

This is an early version of the plot-plan for my first western, *Death at Bethesda Falls*:

Jim Thorp – James Dexter Thorp – is seeking out Clyde Comstock.

On arrival in Bethesda Falls, he tangles with Tom Durey who is mistreating his horse. Takes his whip to the man and gets an enemy for life... [Have your hero or heroine being kind to animals and you've won over quite a few readers.]

Anna Comstock, the schoolteacher, is Clyde's younger sister... Jim and Anna were friends in their childhood.

Clyde is working for Joseph Maxwell as ranch foreman.

Maxwell isn't aware that Clyde is wanted in Kansas for robbing a bank. Anna is aware, however, though she doesn't know the full details.

When Thorp turns up, Anna pleads with him to give Clyde a chance, for old times' sake. She explains that Clyde told her he was involved in a small robbery in Hope Springs but nobody was hurt. He had to leave but anonymously he mailed money each month to repay what was stolen. She believes him.

Thorp doesn't believe the story but hasn't the heart to say so. He won't tell her any details or even that he's a bounty hunter. The bank teller, Oren Sturgess, was shot and slain; a woman and her daughter were trampled to death and a witness was shot too. Thorp has hunted down the other two robbers, Jake Long and

Will Hanson. Before each one died, he told Thorp what happened. There's only Clyde and Ike Douglas left…

Thorp: I can't make that promise, Anna…

She slams the door on him. Anna's drawn between loyalty to her brother and what in her heart she knows is right…

While Thorp settles into his boarding-house room, Anna goes out to the Maxwell ranch – and has strong words with Clyde. And Clyde lets slip that maybe someone was killed, but it wasn't his fault, an accident…

She now understands why Clyde had to leave Hope Springs in a hurry and why they kept moving around. She leaves in tears.

Clyde says that his sister is a great pain; she needs a man to take charge of her. Why won't some man take her so she no longer bothers him as if she were his conscience?

Two men – Abe Dodds and Ed Nash – overhear and fancy getting into the foreman's good books so they follow and then waylay Anna.

Thorp saves her, uses his bullwhip to disarm both men; they have a stand-up fight and Thorp gives them both a good beating before they skulk off.

Thorp explains that he couldn't rest after talking with her and went back to her home and saw her leave on her horse. He got his horse and followed her trail. Caught up to her on return. Just in time.

Now he escorts Anna back to her schoolhouse. 'We'll inform the sheriff in the morning…'

Thorp is roused out of bed in the early hours by Sheriff Latimer who is with the rancher, Maxwell. Maxwell wants Thorp jailed for beating-up his two men…!

Although reluctant, the sheriff arrests Thorp. As he's loath to explain about last night until he has spoken to Anna, Thorp keeps quiet about the circumstances of the fight.

Chow time at the jail. Anna bursts in. She has heard about the arrest. Anxious. Clyde has up and left his job. What have you been keeping from me, Jim?

Through the bars Jim explains about the robbery and the deaths. I was ashamed to tell you I'm a bounty hunter. Clyde's the last man I'll ever hunt.

Sheriff overhears. Decides to let Thorp go. If Maxwell turns up, I'll tell him something. Now, git!

Thorp leaves with Anna. Which way? Towards the sawmill... Anna insists she must go with him.

At the sawmill, they find the owner, James Fitzgerald, lying half-conscious. Three men – one of them Clyde – broke in and tore up the mill house floorboards. Took out two metal chests and stole the buckboard. Headed in the direction of Corrigan Pass. Going towards the prospecting town of Rapid Creek.

They ride hard and spot the single rider and two men on a buckboard trailing two horses. Thorp and Anna are seen and the buckboard veers west towards the waterfall. They're splitting up! The sole rider going north, heading for the pass.

Clyde's with the buckboard. Follow him!

Five natural arches, wonderful sight. Beyond, the Black Hills... Series of waterfalls. Buckboard goes over a narrow road behind the middle waterfall. There's a water-pool and then another drop, the final waterfall... As Thorp and Anna round a bend, a shot is fired through the waterfall curtain – and Anna falls off her horse.

Thorp quickly dismounts and gathers the horses. Anna is all right; the horse's ear was clipped. They find concealment behind some boulders and a few trees. Clyde shouts concern for his sister, blames his accomplice, Abe.

She's all right, no thanks to you!

Anna calls, There's no way through for that wagon!

Thorp: So why would they bring it here? Shots from behind them. The other rider – Ed – had doubled back. They were trapped!

Let my sister come out and she won't be harmed. But however

way you play it, Thorp, you're a goner.

Both Thorp and Anna ride their horses into the pool and over the edge, plummeting down the small waterfall. Shots are fired in vain.

Clearwater River. Their horses survive. They swim downriver for a spell until they can find a shallow area on the eastern bank to get on to dry land. Shaking. Angry. Thorp lost his whip and hat in the river, Anna lost an earring.

They'll bring the buckboard out again and go through Corrigan Pass.

We need dry clothes. Night is coming.

They'll camp in the mountains.

We could go back to town, change and be out on their trail before first light...

Riding into town, wet and dejected. I'll go get my things from Ma McCall's, he says. She goes on to the schoolhouse. Tying up his horse, Thorp is suddenly attacked by a whip snaking round his neck, pulling him back on to the street. Tom Durey wants his revenge. Whip lashes out again. Thorp rolls away from his horse. Durey follows, enjoying himself. His back is to Thorp's horse. Thorp whistles as the whip cracks again and suddenly the horse's hind legs thudded into Durey's back. My horse don't take too kindly to bullies with whips neither. Thorp uses his gun butt to knock Durey out. I'll take that – Durey's whip. Moments later, Sheriff Latimer is on the scene.

If you want to lock him up, be my guest, Sheriff. You might want to raise a posse.

Yeah, heard from James Fitzgerald – mill owner. He's back home being nursed by his missus. I intend to arrange a posse first thing tomorrow.

Fine, we'll leave a good trail for you.

We?

Miss Comstock and me. She wants to save her brother from his just desserts, I reckon...

Having changed into dry clothes, Thorp leads his horse up the street towards the schoolhouse.

Anna opens the door for him. Won't people talk? he asks.

I've got a bank robber for a brother and he almost killed my neighbour, Mr Fitzgerald. I don't think I need worry about an old friend staying for a few hours under my roof!

He gets himself comfortable on the couch... but four hours later she finds him on the floor, fast asleep. Gently she shakes him and he smiles up at her. Now that's a welcome sight, he says. During the fighting, there's many a morning when I pictured your face, just like that... Sometimes, I thought it might be the last time...

Hand on his lips, she says, Shush. No talk of that now.

Breakfast then they saddled up and were off. He's carrying Durey's whip. About an hour before sunup.

Easy enough to follow the fresh wheel tracks. The pass was narrow, just wide enough for two wagons to pass each other with about an inch either side to spare. On the other side, the trail rose steadily. As did the sun, which was just as well, as the going got more treacherous. Narrower in parts, only room for one wagon to pass.

About two hours after sunup they found the buckboard. The two metal chests were there, opened with keys. So they clearly belonged to Clyde, he wasn't stealing them.

His ill-gotten gains.

He didn't post money back, she says, did he?

Nope. Always was a liar, your Clyde.

She glared and then softened. He didn't like you.

Nor me him.

Anna: But you tolerated him to see me?

Yeah. It was worth it...

Anna pulls up, anxious. Thorp says, We should wait for Sheriff Latimer and his posse. You're not safe; they won't hesitate to shoot you, even if you are Clyde's sister.

She can see that Thorp is keen to go on, though, so she agrees to wait for the posse. Just promise you won't kill Clyde...

I'll bring him back alive. I promise. That was one promise it was going to be hard to keep.

Tracking the three fugitives... Suddenly he is pinned down. His faithful horse is shot from under him. It's in pain; he puts it out of its misery. He makes his way through the boulders and closes in on Ed. Where's the posse?

Shooting from behind now but it sounded like an army – or a Gatling gun – pinning down the posse! Where was Anna – in the crossfire?

Abe has skirted round the top of the pass and missed seeing Thorp. Then he heard Ed pin him down and was content. Abe kills two posse members and wounds two more. They skedaddle. The woman, Clyde's sister, was hiding in some rocks. He fired some more to frighten her. Come out or I'll pulverise the whole rock face and you with it!

Tentatively Anna steps out from concealment.

Thorp kills Ed and finds Ed's horse tethered, the saddlebags full of banknotes and jewels.

A horse rider gallops back through the pass, towards Anna... Thorp gives chase.

Abe has the Gatling levelled on Anna. Tells her to come closer. Take off your hat and bandana.

She does so. Gritted teeth.

If you're good to me, I might let you live. Take off your shirt. Go to hell! I'd rather die!

Not very school-marmish, now, is that? Fires at the ground and she jumps back, frightened. That's better. You don't want to die. It ain't worth dyin' for, you know?

Clyde gallops up to Abe and shrieks, What are you doing?

Having a little fun. You said you wanted her to have a man, well, now you get your wish.

Oh, God, then it was you – and Ed...? Then Thorp rides up

and shoots Abe's hand holding the Gatling; he drops it.

Clyde shoots Thorp who is unhorsed. He starts to get up to face Clyde but Anna rushes in front of Thorp, shouting, Clyde, don't do this!

Too late, Clyde shoots his sister and as she falls beside Thorp, he shrieks, Oh, God, what have I done?

Thorp snarls, The last thing you'll ever do! And shoots Clyde dead.

Anna is only wounded.

As they ride back to Bethesda, she says she can't easily wipe out the thought of Thorp killing her brother. He understands. Give it time. He rides away; he won't tell her that the woman and daughter Clyde killed in the robbery were his ma and sister...

The finished book didn't stick to this plot-plan in every detail, and the ending differed considerably. In fact, if the ending were anything like this early draft plan, I wouldn't include it here. I have later versions of the above, but naturally I don't want to give too much away and spoil the story, should you obtain a copy of the book.

What this illustrates is that it's just a plan, after all. A guide, if you like, to get you writing.

A plot-plan is a working document, and it's in here that such elements as flashbacks and withholding information can be noted for subsequent use. It's in the plot-plan where you can reveal – for your own use – what you'll hold back from the reader, thus creating surprises and twists.

And it's in the plot-plan that you can test the linear shape of your storyline – is it going to be strictly chronological or will it go back and forth in time via memories and or flashbacks? Those flashbacks need to be consistent and logical, which can create a headache if you're not careful – for example, revealing something before it actually happened! *Old Guns* begins in 1892 but deals with extensive flashbacks to 1859 and 1866.

Note how the dialogue in the plot-plan isn't in quotation

marks. The characters are speaking directly as the plot is devised. Some phrasing will be kept in the final draft, while others will be embellished or excised as the situation dictates. It doesn't have to be grammatical, either. It's a brain-dump, a word-picture storyboard, subject to change.

The plot-plan sits there while you write your story. Behind your back, without you knowing it, the thing gestates and will require change and improvement as the story goes on, as the characters flesh out and interact.

That's the most exciting aspect of writing – discovering that your characters take on a life of their own to such an extent that they shape much of the plot for you – despite what you've planned.

Gestation

Gestation periods don't count towards your 30 days. The story's happening in your head; you're not sitting at the computer. That's why it's never a good idea to rush off a novel and then immediately send it in the post or through the ether. Indeed, electronic submission makes that option far too easy – missing the vital gestation period – and the submissions editor finds he's then besieged with additional updates afterwards; believe me, I'm speaking from experience.

Let the finished story settle for a few days. It should still be buzzing in your head. Let it.

Often, during this gestation period, certain plot points surface in your mind and you find more dramatic ways to sort these. This happened for me with the denouement in the silver mine in *The $300 Man*, and it happened with the confrontation at the end of *Death at Bethesda Falls*.

Formula

Yes, there are formula plots. They've been used for decades – in books and films. The old westerns from Warner Brothers,

Paramount and others tended to rotate the same storyline between their various franchises. One week Cheyenne was stranded in the desert, the next week it was Maverick, and the week after that, Paladin in *Have Gun Will Travel*.

The silent stranger enters town, shoots the evil mayor, saves the town from the crooked banker and gets the girl but she dies in his arms and he then rides off into the sunset. Next time around, change the names. Change evil saloon owner for evil mayor and crooked sheriff for crooked banker. Next time, change mad cattle baron for evil saloon owner and crooked rail magnate for crooked sheriff. And so on...

There's nothing wrong with formula writing – it has a market. But it's more interesting to steer clear of the obvious and avoid repetition. I'm not that keen on writing in my sleep...

Where formula writing is useful is in series westerns. Here, you have to generate a running storyline over several books. The constant is the hero. The formula: he encounters obstacles to his quest, whatever it is, and overcomes them by the end, then moves on.

Series writing isn't as easy as it seems. It doesn't mean churning out the same old plot time and again. You need to build your fictional world, inhabit it with a varied assortment of characters, and plot not just one book but many, devising a variety of obstacles, ultimately leading to the final book where the hero attains his goal. And you must do all that before you begin writing even the first novel in the sequence.

Getting a publisher interested in a series is a hard sell, and it's unlikely they'd be attracted to your proposal if you haven't already got a history of published work behind you.

Some series characters are written by 'house names' – that is, several authors will use the author name chosen by the publisher.

Appendix F provides a small list of western series characters. A more complete list can be found at the Western Fiction Review blog (see Chapter 3, Research).

8

Character creation

This chapter covers a lot of ground, naturally, as character means story.

It's a toss-up whether you opt for creating your characters first or write your plot-plan. Sometimes, they go along parallel. I started fleshing out my main characters, investing them with backstory, which helped later with the plot-plan.

I prefer to work on the characters first – then I have an idea how they're going to react in any plot I might devise. Inevitably, the character list and descriptions will grow as the story progresses.

Again, there's no definitive way to create a character. If the western has a romantic thriller theme, then the hero may be an Alpha male – or the hero might be a heroine who lives for her work as the widow-boss of a ranch and has no time for romance... until the stranger rides in. Whatever the theme, your main characters – good and bad – should perhaps be a little larger than life and memorable at least for the duration of the book. Give them recognizable traits or features, for example.

As your western has to be set in the past, build up a brief timeline to cover the life of the character, so you know what external influences might affect him or her.

The timeline I used for *The $300 Man*:

Timeline
Books published – Mark Twain, *Roughing It* (1872); George Catlin, *My Life Among the Indians* (1867); stories of Bret Harte – 'The Luck of Roaring Camp' (1868) and 'The Outcasts of Poker Flat' (1869).
1860 – Pony Express begins – ended 1861; transcontinental

telegraph line completed.

1861 – Kansas admitted to the Union.

1866 – Texan ranchers Goodnight and Loving begin trail to Northern Plains; Fetterman Massacre.

1867 – 35,000 cattle driven up Chisholm Trail to Abilene, Kansas; Alaska purchased from Russia.

1868 – Custer and 7th Cavalry massacre Black Kettle's Cheyenne near Washita River, Indian Territory.

1869 – Transcontinental railroad completed; Wyoming extends franchise to women.

1871 – Marshal Wild Bill Hickok kills gunfighter/gambler Phil Coe in Abilene.

1872–73 – Modoc War. 165 Indians led by Captain Jack stand off superior numbers of US army until final capitulation after many pitched battles.

Time of story: July 1874.

Not all of these books or events were used in the novel. Whatever timeline details you sift out, they too need not appear in their entirety. But it helps you get some historical perspective.

Remember, your characters may be adult when they're first introduced to the reader. But they've had a past, and doubtless that past will have shaped them. Hence my timeline goes back earlier than 1874.

One novel I was editing a while ago mentioned the Pony Express, but that legendary means of communication was short-lived and wasn't operating later than 1861, several years before the story I was editing.

Names

The character names may change as the story progresses.

Sometimes, the name just seems to fit. Sister Rose in my thriller *Pain Wears No Mask* was originally Sister Hannah, as it was a Biblical name; but as that was also our daughter's name, I thought I'd better alter it, considering the trauma the character suffered!

Leon Cazador evolved before he appeared in any of the stories to be found in *Spanish Eye*. Cazador, Spanish for 'hunter', seemed very apt. Leon is a strong masculine name, Spanish for 'lion'. As he hunts evil people, it seemed just right.

Corbin Molina, the hooked hero of *The $300 Man*, didn't get his name straight away. It required some thought. One of my many favourite authors is Harlan Coben. Plenty of surnames are also first names in America, so that was sorted. Then I wanted him to be half-Anglo, half-Mexican – just to pile on his problems, since many half-castes were shunned in the West. Actor Alfred Molina played a South American in that excellent biopic *Frida*, which seemed to create a link for me: Molina is a Spanish name, anyway.

Other names were not so easy for *The $300 Man*. In the western books, I try to avoid using the same name, whether it's a minor character or a main one. So, I keep a list from each book. Common names that crop up and have to be changed include Burt, Slim, Josh and Zeke! I've set three books in Bethesda Falls and have a spreadsheet of all of them – sixty-nine at last count – together with their profession and relationship, if any, with others.

My character Clint Brennan in *Blind Justice at Wedlock* was paying homage to the actor Clint Walker.

Screenwriters tend to steer clear of names that begin with the same letter or are homophones. I'll never understand why Tolkien settled on two villains with the names Sauron and Saruman! So, try to avoid naming characters with similar monikers or even with their names beginning with the same letter.

While in real life you might know three or four Daves, Johns or Mikes, fiction isn't the real world, so take it easy on the reader and don't introduce unnecessary confusion and only use a name once. It's not as if there aren't enough to choose from.

One place to research names is on the Internet. Decide on the character's nationality and key in first names for that country. You'll be surprised at the amount of choice offered, together with meanings. Another place is the *Dictionary of First Names* or equivalent books; just make sure that the names you choose are contemporary for the period.

For *The $300 Man*, I used The Civil War Book of Lists, swapping first and surnames around.

Also, you can scan the indexes of non-fiction books about the period and pluck out combinations of appropriate names.

In my list of characters, I covered the period 1860 to 1874. I can then research the books available at the time, the types of weapons and clothes used, and so on.

Some authors use cue cards for their characters – and even for major plot points. It's up to you. I find it useful to set down the date of birth, clothing favoured, weapons, if any, physical appearance, verbal mannerisms, and backstory.

Backstory

Although your story may take place between 1865 and 1899, for example, the characters' lives will have evolved in the past and been affected by their experiences. The trek of many wagon trains from the 1840s, opening the west at great cost, will be part of several characters' past. The Indian Wars, while almost over by the mid 1880s, still impacted the lives of settlers, townspeople and outlaws. The war with Mexico, the influx of immigrants from Europe, the gang culture of New York – all these might affect your characters.

The character's backstory will grow as they interact; it's rare for the backstory to emerge fully formed. So, even though in my breakdown of characters you'll see more or less complete backstories, they didn't start like that; they were added to as I went along, much like the plot-plan.

Minor characters

While minor characters don't need as much description, it's useful to give each of them some identifying feature, whether the hair colour or nose shape. Or a humorous trait. If a barkeep simply serves the drink, don't dwell on him too much; if however he has information to divulge to our taciturn stranger in town, then imbue the barkeep with a little more life.

Here are a few character descriptions from *The $300 Man*:

Corbin Molina

Born – 5 January, 1846 (16 in 1862, 21 in 1867, 28 in 1874).

Half-breed – half-Mexican, half-Anglo.

Clothing

Fawn buckskin jacket, long, thigh-high.

Dark blue flannel shirt.

Cavalry trousers, with yellow stripe down outside leg.

Black slouch hat.

Weapons

Winchester rifle, 15 rounds, .44-40 centre-fire.

Frontier Colt single-action .44 (manually cock, accurate up to 50 yds).

Physical appearance

Sun-tanned dark complexion, leathery neck, broad square shoulders.

Almond-shaped eyes. Deep brown eyes, slightly hooded.

Skewed nose, crooked, having been broken at least once.

Square jaw, heavy dark eyebrows.

Rugged body, 6 ft.

Chiselled abdomen.

Black hair with a white streak on left, over small scar on forehead; long, hanging to bottom of earlobes.

Left hand missing, replaced by metal box to which implements can be clipped. Adaptable implements on belt include a fork, a knife, a hook, a spike and a clamp. The contraption's held on by a metal brace and leather straps to shoulder and upper arm.

Verbal mannerisms

Husky voice, sometimes soothing.

Backstory

Birth mother was Paloma Molina. Taken in by Jubal Buford when his ma died. Fighting for the Union, he was conspicuously brave in battle, but lost a hand during the attack on Fort Fisher, Wilmington. When he was discharged, he learned to use his hook. Then he went home. But the family had up and left.

Jubal Buford

Rich rancher. Has a son, Sam and wife, Lydia.

Born – 6 June, 1814 (48 in 1862).

Backstory

Loved first wife, Eliza, who died when giving birth to Clara, who also died 3 days later (May, 1840). He realized he'd made a mistake in marrying Lydia when she gave birth to Sam. Afterwards, she lived for the boy, not him. Jubal was her means to an end, it seemed. She withdrew her love so he strayed to Paloma who worked in the town canteen. Sired Corbin. When Paloma died and Corbin was only 3 years old, Jubal insisted they take in the boy. On one condition, he would be a 'distant relative' and live in the bunkhouse, not the ranch house. Jubal agreed, and the marriage soured even more so. His heart went out to the young boy, but he dared not tell the lad who his father was; it was a secret between him, the doctor and his wife. Even Sam didn't know the truth. He worried about Sam; he was too darned close to his ma.

Sam Buford/Samuel Walker

Born – 10 March, 1844 (18 in 1862, 23 in 1867, 30 in '74).

Physical appearance

As an 18 year old, slim-hipped, tall, with thick sandy hair.

As a 30 year old, stout, barrel-chested, with thinning salt-and-pepper hair; also sideburns; middle-aged spread.

Small and round eyes – beady.

Hawk brown eyes – greyish-brown.

Pug nose – short, flattened, turned up at the end.

Protruding lips.

Round firm chin.

Square shoulders.

Verbal mannerisms

Thick, throaty voice – turned more hoarse at 30.

Backstory

Resented the presence of Corbin but hid it whenever his father was around. Manipulated events so that often Corbin was punished for some transgression that Sam had committed. Jubal hated using the strap on Corbin. When the Civil War began, Sam was old enough to volunteer, but he wouldn't; when the draft was imposed, he was called to account. He talked Corbin into being his substitute; 'You can save that $300 for when you return to wed Jean (Pegram),' Sam told Corbin. So, Corbin lied about his age and went off to war in Sam's stead. Sam wooed Corbin's girl Jean and he promised to marry her.

Lydia Buford, née Walker

Born – 9 September, 1826 (41 in 1867, 48 in '74).

Jubal's second wife, married in 1843.

Clothing

Blacks and greys.

Physical appearance

Slight of build, sinewy, but tough. Long-drawn features, grey-flecked black hair, tied back. Alabaster complexion. Gimlet eyes, piercing, penetrating. Eye colour – blueberry; light to medium blue; fiery blue eyes. Small and dainty nose, she considers her worst feature. Plum-coloured lips, sensual sometimes. Round chin approaching double. Small glistening white teeth. Short, almost diminutive yet commanding presence; lean body. Round shoulders. Stubby fingers. Lavishly endowed chest, well-defined hips.

Verbal mannerisms

Cultured voice, sometimes lilting. When angered, scabrous voice.

Backstory

She set her cap at Jubal as he was one of the wealthiest available men in the county. Over the years she wore down Jubal and when Jubal insisted on housing and feeding his whelp, she grasped her chance. She used Corbin's presence to wheedle whatever she wanted out of Jubal. She was too close to her son Sam and saw to it that Corbin's life was a misery whenever possible. Finally, when the draft notice came, she told Sam what to do. Corbin left without telling Jubal where he was going. It broke the old man's heart. He died six months later. Lydia and Sam sold up and headed west where they knew their wealth would establish them as people of means and power. They were accompanied by Jean, who was still waiting to be married to Sam. This displeased Lydia. Halfway to their destination, they stopped over in a small town (Retribution) and after a flaming row Lydia got her way and sold off Jean to the bordello for a nice little sum. 'You can't afford to have a woman and mewling brats till you've made your fortune, son,' she told him. He went along with that. They'd be an encumbrance. They found the beginnings of a small town and changed their name to Walker, Lydia's maiden name; with his mother behind him, Samuel Walker proved an astute businessman and profiteered from the war. They started small and inside three years, with her guidance, the

Walkers had built up the small town, renamed it Walkerville; she wasn't going to grace the place with her late husband's name, no sir.

Malinda Dix

Born – 24 October, 1838 (24 in 1862, 29 in 1867, 36 in '74).

Clothing

Greys and dark greens, unpretentious.

Physical appearance

Complexion that reminded him of hay – golden brown, silky smooth. Strawberry birthmark on her left temple. Sloe eyed – large and dark or almond-shaped. Eye colour – autumn leaf/reddish brown with a hint of yellow. A high distinctive bridge to her nose, high forehead, square chin. Hair – burnt almond, long, frizzy when wet; tied back in a bun when working. Quite thick firm generous rosy-red lips. Pearly teeth. Ethereal face in certain lighting conditions. Dimpled cheeks and eyes mirthful crescents when laughing/grinning. Full rounded figure, firm waist and hips. Slender neck, delicate shoulders, belying strength of her arms. Melon-breasted. Long, delicate hands, clipped nails.

Verbal mannerisms

Soothing voice, sometimes velvety, sometimes sultry; well bred.

Backstory

Nurse and practising doctor during Civil War. Started out helping the newly-established relief association. The surgeon was not like many of the rest, he appreciated her quick mind and skilled hands – before long, she was performing major surgery and, sadly, many an amputation. Towards the end of the war, Captain Corbin Molina was brought in to her and she had to amputate his left hand. He adapted well and seemed much more mature than his years. Later, she meets him again...

Jean Pegram – Jeannie

Born – 7 July, 1847 (15 in 1862, 18 in 1867, 27 in '74).

Clothing

Green silk pelisse; calico dress; jacket bodice and skirt; mantle – sleeveless coat.

Physical appearance

Alabaster complexion; used to be freckled as a child.

Hollowed eye sockets, malnourished. Hazel eyes, nose turned up at the tip – has been broken and reset. Copper-coloured hair, long. Oval face, puckered lips. Pearly teeth, but one missing at side. Willowy. Long fingers. Breasts – jutting cones.

Verbal mannerisms

Throaty, tremulous voice. Demure giggle.

Backstory

Once-girlfriend of Corbin. A bit of a tomboy, she played with both Corbin and Sam. She thought she was in love with Corbin, but when he came to her on his last night and told her he was going to fight in the war, and she was to wait for him, she wept into her pillow and decided she would not fret for him or wait. She was also pleased that Sam showed a stronger interest in her. When he promised to marry her, she gave in to his overtures. Trouble was, he never did marry her. She heard later that it was his mother who made the financial arrangements with the madam of the brothel in Retribution. She could try to escape, but the threat was very real – recapture and severe punishment; a stick to the soles of her feet. She'd seen Monica hobbling for weeks after she received that treatment. 'We don't aim to stop you working, honey,' the madam told her. 'You can still lie down and earn, but you sure as hell won't be able to run away!' She had lost her self-respect and stayed.

Jeremiah Hood

Born – 29 November, 1845 (19 in 1862, 24 in 1867, 29 in '74).

Bounty jumper. Now a drunk in Retribution – was thrown out of Walkerville by sheriff.

Clothing – 'tattered shirt'

'His clothes were torn and filthy; a draught through the entrance informed Corbin that the man could do with a bath, too. He'd seen enough hobos to know that beneath all that grime was a man years younger than he appeared; now, he looked about forty.'

Motivation

As can be seen in the samples of backstory, there are several instances where character motivation has been embedded. People generally don't do something without a reason. They're motivated by pride, greed, altruism, love, anger, jealousy, hate and a lot more besides.

Lydia hates Mexicans, because her husband found love and solace in a Mexican woman's arms. The child of that union was Corbin, of course – so she doesn't like him, either – his mixed race is a constant affront to her. So her past shapes how she feels towards the Mexican workers at the silver mine. Her past provides her with powerful motivation for her current actions and intent.

Certainly, incidents or people in their past might return to haunt them. By building a past for your characters, they cease to be made of cardboard. Within a short while, they'll seem alive.

Somerset Maugham has said that every action of a character must be the result of a definite cause – significantly related to the entire fiction, of course.

Each motive must be in keeping with the character's behaviour pattern that you've established. Otherwise, you lose credibility.

Conflict

Without conflict of some kind, there is no story. The conflict doesn't have to be life or death – but it must test your hero or heroine to the utmost. How the protagonist rises above the conflict emphasises that character's major emotional trait.

Each test must be a crisis – a critical time in the protagonist's life.

There have to be obstacles in the character's way, making the test difficult.

Your characters *must* be in conflict – whether with their consciences, their families or neighbours or the antagonist.

Conflict types:

Supernatural

Human

Other entities – animals, wildlife etc.

Non-living entities – things and objects of every kind

Natural forces – time, the elements, disease

Social forces – economic conditions, politics, morality, religion etc.

Inner self – conscience, belief system, loyalties and repressed self

All of the above conflict types can be used in a western – yes, even the supernatural!

That conflict keeps the pages turning. Introduce conflict of some kind early and pile it on throughout the book, saving the greatest obstacle for the end.

In the first paragraph of the Prologue in *The $300 Man*, the protagonist Corbin Molina is faced with serious conflict. He's being robbed at gunpoint on a train.

Naturally, I wanted Corbin's hook to be seen by the reader as soon as possible, so I managed that in the second slightly long paragraph.

Perched on the edge of his aisle seat on the right-hand side of the swaying railway carriage, Corbin was coiled like a spring, biding his time, ready to jump the robbers. The money didn't concern him too much; it was the opened envelope Granger had taken with the cash: if the train-robber read the letter inside, he'd more than likely shoot Corbin where he sat. A thin-lipped smile was the only expression on his reddish-brown features as he held his arms aloft, the left terminating in a stump encased by a metal band and brandishing a hook. Further up the carriage was a forest of upheld arms. Corbin's hooded deep brown eyes glared past his hat brim at the train-robber he'd recognised.

'Hey, don't look at me like that, Mister.' As Bert spoke he revealed two broken teeth; his voice was high-pitched, as if his unmentionables had been trapped in a vice. 'This may be a lot of greenbacks, but it sure as hell ain't worth dying for!'

'I don't think this is the time or place to discuss the economics of a life,' Corbin said ruefully, his voice husky, 'though I have my own firm opinion on the subject.' (pp. 5/6)

Note also that I've adopted an omniscient point of view at this early stage to describe the hero, Corbin – 'reddish-brown features', 'thin-lipped smile', and his arms aloft, the 'left one terminating in a stump encased by a metal band and brandishing a hook.' Also, his 'hooded deep brown eyes' glared.

We finally leap into Corbin's POV on the next page, where we read his thoughts. From then on, when he's in the scene, it's usually – though not always – his POV.

Although the two train robbers are minor characters and die very soon, they're important to the atmosphere of the scene, so they're described through their dialogue and Molina's observations. Don't skimp on your minor characters, but don't go overboard, either. Of course the Granger gang's motivation is simple enough: greed.

I end the prologue with the hint of retribution to come from the surviving Granger brother – in a subtle switch to the alarmed widow's POV.

The widow fanned herself and tried to concentrate on the

passing barren country. Her eyes widened for a second as their carriage passed a man mounted on a piebald at the edge of the permanent way's embankment. He was holding the reins of two other horses and there was a look of puzzlement on his face, as if he'd been expecting the train to stop for him. (p. 10)

Romance

A number of first-time readers of western novels express surprise when they encounter romance in the storyline. Why the surprise? It's part of the human condition, after all.

The character of Dr Malinda Dix didn't figure in the first rough plot-plan. But as I approached the flashback of the Civil War and sketched out Corbin losing his hand, I thought I'd try to be slightly different and use a female doctor.

Research checks confirmed that it was feasible, as women doctors were not unheard of in the Old West. Jefferson Davis commissioned Ms Sally Tompkins of Richmond as a captain of cavalry in the Confederate Army in 1861. Her hospital, which she established after the battle of the First Bull Run, proved to have a remarkably high recovery rate. Doctors Sarah Clapp and Mary Walker were commissioned as contract surgeons in the Union Army. The names of Malinda and Dix came from two individuals in *The Book of Civil War Lists*.

Dorothea Dix, aged 59, set up a nurses' corps against official opposition. She was referred to as 'Dragon Dix'. She advertised for nurse recruits, emphasising that they must be 'plain looking and at least thirty years old. Those wearing jewellery need not apply.' Her nurse recruits worked for nothing, then Congress authorised 40c per day plus meals and transportation. Julia S. Wheelock, 29, of the Michigan Soldiers' Relief Association said, 'I could not think of him as a rebel, he was too near Heaven for that.' These nurses could provide fascinating backstories.

I then decided there would be a romance between Malinda and Corbin – and then the idea of them both being fond of poetry popped into my head. So the moral of this is, don't over-plan everything. Let the characters breathe – and sometimes they'll show you what they want.

The plot-plan was subsequently updated.

Violence

A western without violence is almost an oxymoron. However, there are a few to be found. Prolific author Frank Roderus' trilogy about Harrison Wilke is a case in point: *Leaving Kansas* (1983), *Reaching Colorado* (1984) and *Finding Nevada* (1985). Not a shot is fired in any of these books. Basically decent and generous people, extolling what is best in the human spirit, populate Roderus' West.

So, the concern isn't the presence of violence, it's the depth of description involved. For example, Robert Hale doesn't like to see graphic violence against women in their westerns. I'd planned an ambush in *The $300 Man* and initially wrote a graphic death scene; then I reviewed it and realized I didn't have to go so far. Often, only a few words are necessary; less is more:

She screamed, her mouth wide, the sound rebounding from the ancient stones.

'Stop that caterwauling, woman!' he shouted, but she ignored him.

Slowly, methodically, all four men fired at her, taking their time. And the gulch echoed with the shots and the air was clogged with gun smoke and the stink of sudden death. (p. 66)

Fights of any sort can become tedious to the reader if the antagonists don't have identities. *The one-eyed man hit the curly-haired guy on the head with a bottle.*

Another problem is giving a nameless character lots of various descriptions, such as the intruder, the tall man, the attacker, the Indian, and so on – yet they're all describing the same person. This just confuses the reader and at one point he or she might wonder who's that 'tall man', where'd he come from?

Try to weave in their names before the action, perhaps by addressing each other by name.

Long descriptions in violent scenes slow down the reader, which you definitely don't want in a western! I've seen a single paragraph of action of over thirty lines of text, where the two main characters are battling it out, and it's so easy to get lost in there. A different action virtually always calls for a new paragraph. Short tightly written paragraphs read faster than thick ones.

Some beginning writers will give a man a name then not use it, rather going for 'the thin man in black' or 'the scarred man'. They're neglecting POV, as outlined in Chapter 5, subheading *Action*. If the hero, for example, knows the name of his antagonist, he'll think of him with that name. *Curly swung an axe, but Jake ducked and pivoted on his heel...*

Sex

Yes, there's sex in western novels. It can vary, depending on the publisher and the market. This example is relatively mild, but conveys enough without being too graphic.

'Tomorrow, honey, it will all be over,' Corbin said, cupping her melon-shaped breasts and kissing them. A light scent of lemon verbena clung to her skin.

'It's a dangerous game you play,' she whispered, running a finger over the welts in his shoulder.

'With you – or the Walkers?'

'Oh, the Walkers. This is no game we play, darling Corbin. This is serious.' She kissed him and for the second time this night they made love, though now it was languorous and not a frenzied catching up of lost years.

(*The $300 Man*, p. 136)

Just sufficient visual information to aid the reader, with the addition of scent; the senses aroused.

Indeed, there's a rather large market for Adult Westerns. You can spot them easily enough – their covers feature scantily clad women. These aren't too reticent where sadistic violence and graphic sex are concerned and will feature expletives as well. The label is a bit annoying, as the vast majority of westerns are adult in theme and treatment, though without the preponderance of sex, violence and swearing.

Swearing

The other day, an author I work with expressed concern when a reader castigated her over her use of swearing in her book. I pointed out that expletives had become commonplace since the 1980s. Sure, they were around before then, but not in such number to the point where they now seem all pervasive.

I recall the minor furore when Dick Francis first used the F-word. I'll refrain from spelling out the various examples. Francis probably lost a few readers in libraries, but otherwise his inclusion of expletives didn't affect his sales. Lincoln Child's debut novel *The Relic* was spoiled in my view by the profusion of 'in character' expletives, yet the book helped the writing duo embark on a successful career. While s*** and f*** are now commonly used in books, there's still a certain reluctance to use c***. In my library of reference books, I've got *The Dictionary of Contemporary Slang* and *The Thesaurus of American Slang*: there are plenty of more colourful variations for insults and swear words. But beware of anachronisms even in slang and swearing.

So, putting expletives in your characters' mouths is really a gut decision. If you're not comfortable about it, there are alternatives. You simply type: 'He swore.' Or variants of that. The reader still gets the message. For my Leon Cazador crime short stories (collected in *Spanish Eye*), I simply wrote, 'He swore colourfully,' or whatever, since the stories appeared in magazines and children or a maiden aunt could easily pick them up. And this is the approach I have to my western novels too.

You'll probably find that most western purists prefer little or no profanity and expletives. This is perhaps where you have to do your market research. If the publisher you're aiming at doesn't publish western novels that feature swearing, be assured they won't want your submission to attempt to 'push the envelope'.

And remember, if you opt for swearing, make sure it's appropriate for the period.

But what is the purpose of swearing? It can be seen as a lack of vocabulary. Some use it as punctuation and don't even know they're doing it. As someone said, 'Once the expletives were deleted, he didn't say much.' A character swears because he's exasperated, is in mortal danger, hurt, wishes to insult or is alarmed. It can be used as a pressure valve, to release tension, too. Whatever the reason, I feel that in writing that book or story, swearing should be used sparingly, to convey shock or other emotions; so yes, I used the F-word nine times in my crime thriller about the crime-fighting nun Sister Rose.

Indeed, in the real world expletives are as commonplace as those *ums* and *ers* with which people pepper their speech. But as writers we're not writing the real world, we're creating the impression of a real world – a different thing entirely.

My late father was in the army during WWII and was wounded in Sicily. I never heard him swear. Maybe he did, but clearly not in front of women or children.

At least, since you're contemplating writing a western, there's some guidance. The so-called Code of the West has this to say: 'Cuss all you want... but only around men, horses and cows.' I know, it would appear that the writers and producers of *Deadwood* ignored that code. And George Sicking said, 'Real cowboys are tough but not vulgar. You can tell them by the way they treat women. If a man doesn't respect women enough to clean up his mouth, he doesn't respect himself.' That's not a bad credo to live by, in my book.

Humour

Life isn't always serious. Sometimes, humour is necessary to get through the day. Like life, like fiction. Inject humour into your characters – not all the time, obviously, unless it's going to be a comic western novel, of which there are too few. One such is Bill Pronzini's *The Last Days of Horse-Shy Halloran* (1987); another is Jack Martin's *Wild Bill Williams* (2012).

Humour can be ironic, slapstick, witty or farcical in parts, since real life isn't all one tone; it's light and dark, with highs and lows.

For some obscure reason, most editors and publishers fight shy of puns. A notable exception seems to be George G. Gilman's Edge series. For example, in his *Arapaho Revenge* (1983) each chapter ends with a play on words, and on occasion a cringe-worthy pun!

Of course, you need to know when to use the humour. It can unintentionally deflate a tense or dramatic moment.

Continuity

Film-makers have a continuity person – to make sure the actor is holding the cup in the same hand for each fresh take, is wearing the dress in the same manner as earlier, and so on, among other important minor details. When you're writing your western, you're the continuity person. You can't rely on an editor checking the continuity for glitches. It's up to you. And no, we'll never get everything right – there are too many balls being juggled at the same time. But, at least, try to spot continuity hiccups.

For example, don't mislay a character. On occasion, a minor character is introduced and is travelling with the posse, but he never speaks, never contributes, and to all intents and purposes might as well not be there; indeed, the reader can't *see* him, so he isn't there!

The same applies to animals. I've read where a dog jumps in to save the hero, and as far as the writer was concerned, the dog had been with the hero all the time, but the reader wasn't privy to that information, and didn't *see* the dog, so it seemed like the dog jumped in out of the blue, a contrived *deus ex machina*.

In westerns, characters get wounded. Make sure you remember that – which arm was pierced with an arrow? Did he get his arm put in a sling? How'd he manage that fistfight with one arm incapacitated? Simple, the author forgot about the wound that happened a dozen pages back. The hero was wounded in the left leg, but after a few pages he forgets to limp – or he limps on the wrong leg.

So, where continuity is concerned, get it right when you write.

9

Get writing

Naturally, if I'm advocating writing a western novel in thirty days, writers want to know how they achieve this target, day by day.

There is no magic wand. I can list what is required, however:

Discipline

Without this, you won't achieve your target. Many would-be novel writers have several novels in the early stages, gathering dust. But they haven't finished any of them. No staying power. Stay with your plot-plan. You have to, to finish the book.

Many novelists say the best way to write is to place your bum on the seat and apply pen to paper or finger to keyboard.

Having said that, it's very tempting to find some excuse *not* to work, not to write. Even successful writers will procrastinate and find excuses to avoid writing. Housework, answering correspondence, doing those dreadful jobs you'd normally put off; whatever the task, it seems preferable to staring at a blank sheet of paper and filling it up with meaningful words.

Take H.G. Wells, for example. He said, 'There comes a moment in the day, when you have written your pages in the morning, attended to your correspondence in the afternoon, and have nothing further to do. Then comes the hour when you are bored: that's the time for sex.'

Of course he had quite a reputation, conducting a number of liaisons while married, including two other women giving birth to his daughter and son. His novel *Ann Veronica* caused a sensation when it was published in 1909. Clearly, he enjoyed female company as much as his writing!

The vast majority of writers cannot stop, no matter what.

Aileen Armitage started writing in the 1960s and has over thirty books published, many written while her eyesight gradually failed, and she is still writing. There's always something to say, some character to invent, it seems.

Isaac Asimov said that if he was told he only have six months to live, he'd have to type faster. (He was fast anyway, having written 463 books by the time he died aged seventy-two – science fiction, mystery, and popular science, among others.)

Self-belief

You can do it. Persevere. The schedule isn't an albatross around your neck, it's an aid, to keep you motivated.

Be confident. The more you write, the better you become.

Focus

Don't wander from the main thrust of your story. It's very easy to get wrapped up in research or let your characters lead you in unplanned directions. Resist these blandishments.

Stay focussed. Your plot-plan will help you with this.

Writer's block

Tell yourself there's no such thing. If you're stuck in a certain point of your plot-plan, then go forward to another part of the story and build that, and return to your 'blocked' section later.

That's the beauty of a plot-plan – you've got other places to go, while the back of your head – the subconscious – sorts out your problem; and it usually does.

Day 1

Be honest with yourself. Don't beaver away and skip entering some of that time on your spreadsheet.

First day should be about creating your main character(s) and jotting down the beginning of the plot-plan. I don't include research time in my schedule.

However, when I make research notes, I tend to insert the fact in my spreadsheet, but they don't count against the number of days' writing.

Of course, the research notes can be inserted into the plot-plan at any salient point. The time spent updating the plot-plan *is* counted in the schedule.

So, for *The $300 Man*, the start of the schedule reads:

		Total words
7 May	Character names/plot begun	831
9 May	Begin novel	1029
22 May	Characters built further	365
23 May	Plot enlarged	1673
24 May	Number of words of novel written	381
27 May	Number of words of novel written	1248
28 May	Number of words of novel written	2137

and so on...

As you can see, I didn't work on the novel every day, due to other writing commitments. But I had a schedule and I knew where I was and how much more I had to do to reach my goal, the 45,000-word mark.

Stick to that schedule, using the spreadsheet.

Maintain a record of progress.

Day 2 – and the rest

You're measuring your days in chunks of eight hours. Those hours can be spread over any length of time or consecutively; it's up to your lifestyle and other commitments.

By monitoring your hours, you're keeping to the schedule.

Remember, when an author says he spent years writing his great tome, he doesn't mean he spend every second of every day for years on it. His time spent on it was in chunks, some small, some large.

Try to devote time for an easy-to-work-out session – a minimum of 30-minutes, for example. One day, maybe you'll only work for 1.5 hours – fine; you've got 6.5 hours left in that 'day'.

See Appendix A for a rough breakdown of those thirty days.

Ploys to keep writing

Keep typing and don't stop to worry about holes in the plot that you might have just identified. They can be fixed later. Make a quick note in the plot-plan and then continue to get the words down while the story flows.

The more you write about your characters, the more they'll tell you, even subconsciously. As the characters react to situations you've put them in, they'll reveal traits and behaviour you probably haven't planned in detail. Go with the flow – and update your character list and plot-plan at the earliest opportunity when the flow slows or stops.

Updating your plot-plan and character list will prompt you to get back into the story, too. It can become a cyclic process, and of great benefit.

If you're hitting a slow period – don't despair. Review your earlier pages. Maybe you can add depth to a scene – layering, mentioned later in Chapter 12. Review your plot-plan – have other subplots suggested themselves since you began? If so, investigate them, see if they lead anywhere interesting that will move your story forward; but remember to maintain focus.

Even when you're not writing, in any quiet moment while you're washing the dishes or doing other mundane tasks, mull over your story and characters. You'll be surprised how soon you'll want to be at the computer again, to continue telling your story.

The longer you leave the work alone, the harder it will be to return to it. At least, until you have a few written books under your belt. When you know that you can complete a novel-length story, you'll be more confident about leaving the work in progress alone for a while, and you might not even feel guilty about it. Though those characters you've created – who are in stasis – might start begging you to get on with the rest of *their* story…

Whatever you do, don't abandon the work in progress. Don't be one of those wannabe authors who have drawers full of half-completed manuscripts. Return to that schedule and persevere.

Tinkering

Oscar Wilde stated, 'All morning I worked on the proof of one of my poems, and I took out a comma; in the afternoon, I put it back.'

You can eat up a lot of precious time by simply tinkering – changing a word here, cutting and pasting a paragraph there, bothering over punctuation. Yes, these actions may be necessary – but only when you've finished the book, at the self-edit stage, not while you should be in full flood, pounding the keys to reach your word count target.

Unless you're really stuck for something to write about, avoid tinkering and keep writing.

If you think you've hit a brick wall, tinkering might get the creative juices going and might increase your word count. But only tinker as a last resort for that session.

Maintaining a high word count

It depends how fast you type. If you touch-type, then it will be relatively easy to get those words down in quick fashion. Let's be honest, writing about 1,800 words or so in eight hours is no big deal.

Even a two-finger typist can get a lot of words down in a minute.

If you prefer to use a pen or pencil first and then transfer your words to the computer afterwards, then it will be slower, much slower.

Remember, it's best to write too many words as you get the story down, as you put flesh on the bones of your plot-plan. Self-edit, which we'll come to, will sort out the excessive verbiage and repetitions.

Don't stop to check the number of words done as you pound the keys – just keep going, fleshing out as you go.

Do a word count only at the end of a session.

Criticism

Beginner writers feel cut off to some extent, tied to a desk and a keyboard. Nowadays, there's the Internet and a plethora of writing group sites, many of which solicit samples of work to be critiqued.

I'd advise against seeking a critique of a work in progress – unless you really have hit what seems like a brick wall and you feel really isolated. Generally, fellow authors are generous with their time and comments – whether they're in a local writers' circle or online.

But bear in mind that any reader's opinion is just that – an opinion. It's subjective, not personal, and it might not be an informed opinion.

You're free to take the advice or not. Maybe some suspect plot-point has been spotted, where the internal logic isn't quite right. Great, set about fixing it. If a critique doesn't back up any negative comments with examples, then it's of no real help, so maybe you should discard those comments.

A writer has to have a thick skin. Destructive criticism, sadly, has increased on the Internet, where those carping critics are anonymous. These are people who seem to delight in demolishing someone else's work – even without due reason. Granted, a few wannabe writers might perhaps benefit from somebody advising them that actually they'll never be able to write a good dramatic story, no matter how marvellous the story appears, but that kind of earth-shattering observation should come from a friend, not a stranger.

Constructive criticism is another thing entirely. That must be welcomed, without getting too possessive or precious about your own words. We all make mistakes – no matter how hard we work on the prose, rewriting and self-editing till we reach the point where we want to read something fresh and different. Far better to be advised of any shortcomings before you send the book off to the publisher, believe me!

Partners and other family members generally don't make good critics of your work. There are exceptions, naturally. But unless you can say hand on heart that your spouse, friend, brother, sister, mother, or father is widely read and fully cognizant of dramatic fiction requirements, then you might not get any useful feedback. 'I liked it very much' isn't helpful criticism, though it's a balm to hear.

Daily schedule

At Appendix A, there's a very rough breakdown for days 1–30. By now, you should see that it has to be rough, depending on your productivity per 'day' (i.e. per block of eight hours).

The important thing is to maintain a schedule, something against which you can measure your progress. Without it, you're never going to write – and finish – the book in thirty days. That speaks for itself, really.

10

Dialogue

Speech helps to define your story's characters.

Many beginner writers shun dialogue, because they fear they won't be able to get the characters' words right, or they worry about the speech patterns, jargon or vernacular in a western.

The fact is that dialogue reveals character; it moves the story forward much faster than narrative, and can impart information more economically than several paragraphs of exposition.

Direct speech dramatises events, while indirect speech merely reports them.

The spoken word *engages* the reader.

It's true that some short stories can work without any dialogue at all; very few books can, though. So if you want your story to be believable, you're going to have to handle dialogue – conversation between two or more characters.

The trick is to make the dialogue sound realistic without it being real. Most real-life conversations are interspersed with *ums* and *ahs*, verbal ticks and regional slang – don't use these unless you intend to convey a particular character's verbal mannerisms, and then only do so sparingly, otherwise the reader finds it tedious.

Try to personalise the speech of each character, so that if you didn't spell out who was speaking, it would still be obvious by the tone, vocabulary, content and context. Of course, this isn't always viable, it depends on what is being said; but strive for this effect wherever possible. Perhaps a man who works with his hands talks in a clipped fashion, while a seamstress lady has a more flowery turn of phrase. If you can, get the character to use some terminology from her profession; Tracy Chevalier achieved this brilliantly in her bestseller *Girl with a Pearl Earring* (1999).

There's no reason why a saloon gambler couldn't use references to his profession in his conversation, after all. J.B. Priestley's first person narrator, Tim Bedford, in *Saturn Over the Water* (1961) is an artist and it's obvious because his perception of the world is seen through an artist's eyes.

The dialogue is meant to tell the reader what they need to know about the people, the plot or even the story's theme. To a certain extent, you have more space and freedom in a novel – yet you must keep the dialogue pertinent. Every word should count, should do something towards an end.

Basics

It still surprises me that I receive novel submissions where the author has neglected to follow the publisher's guidelines or has no real idea about punctuation on the page.

Apologies to those who are in the know. For those who aren't sure, it isn't rocket science. I'd advise them that they should study published books to see how dialogue is laid out. Whenever a different person is speaking, that speech should be in a new paragraph. That doesn't mean the paragraph has to start with the speech, however. Wherever appropriate, use some action or description to break up dialogue.

For example:

'Are Mort and Rufus still here?' he asked, his voice husky.

She hunkered down in the bed and drowsily shook her head. 'No, they skedaddled at about the same time as the bank was robbed.' She laughed hollowly, nursing her empty glass. 'Mrs Begley wasn't best pleased, I can tell you!' Smiling at the memory, she fell asleep.

Gently moving off the bed, Corbin took the tumbler out of her hand and pulled the covers over her. (p. 27)

The narrative description or the spoken text can indicate who is speaking.

Also note that if you're using 'he said' or an equivalent, you should end the speech with a comma – unless it ends in a question or an exclamation (as above).

As for quotation marks, usage of the double (") or single (') will depend on your target publisher. Study the market. Don't emulate Cormac McCarthy who eschews speech quotation marks entirely – *All the Pretty Horses* (1992). While he can get away with it, very few other writers can. Make it easy for the reader/publisher.

Also, if you're quoting something within a speech, employ the other quote mark, for example:

'Have you read "The Last of the Mohicans" by James Fennimore Cooper?' he asked.

Or:

"Have you seen the new actress in the show 'Camille'?" he demanded.

When a character's speech is broken into paragraphs, the quotation marks only appear at the beginning of the new paragraph and the closing quotation mark is placed at the end of the entire speech, not the end of that paragraph, like this:

Major Newton sat down at his desk, opened a drawer and extracted a brown folder and riffled through several sheets of paper. 'There's a town called Ashkelon.

'It's in the South, but carpetbaggers and the like have been robbing the few families and landowners blind.

'What with military law and all, they can't rightly fight back, so they just cave in.

'The Confederate survivors are becoming strangers in their

own land. Northern businessmen are buying up or forcing out old firms and businesses.

'It isn't honourable, Corbin. Worse, it's making a mockery of the Reconstruction. It has to stop.' (adapted from p. 95)

Enough said.

Dialogue speaks volumes

Dialogue must move the story forward and reads faster than narrative. As Anthony Trollope said, 'The dialogue must tend in some way to the telling of the story.' Which means, dialogue is there:

- To carry on the plot
- To foreshadow coming conflict
- To reveal character
- To indicate the setting

Never get characters to speak so that it's obvious that they're spoon-feeding the reader with information (that dreaded infodump springs to mind).

Move the story and build up the character with dialogue.

Remember, dialogue is there for a purpose – it isn't just filler – so avoid the 'one lump or two, vicar' kind that tells us nothing.

The way your characters speak should appear natural – without the real *ums* and *ers*. Real speech is not good dialogue. Good dialogue gives the semblance of real speech.

Stilted overformal expressions are usually fatal to dialogue. Naturally, it's possible to have a character who speaks in a particular stilted fashion – that's his characterisation.

The majority of people speak using contractions – I'll, I'm and we've, for example: I am, I will and we have are stilted and again slow down the speech.

Try to make each speech pattern appropriate to the character.

One person might use lengthy sentences with long words, while another will speak in a terse fashion.

Dialogue is always useful where there might be a tendency to POV-switch. Instead of jumping into another character's head and thoughts, get that character to voice his thoughts.

Avoid vernacular. Yes, in short bursts it might be humorous or even character defining, but it can soon wear thin over a novel's length. Don't overdo the truncatin' of words, either. Modern readers don't like to struggle with the meaning of what a character is saying – dialogue should flow and be clear. Besides, vernacular and unusual phrasing slows down the story. Mary Webb's *Gone to Earth* (1917) is a deserved classic, but it wouldn't be a runaway bestseller now – its vernacular makes it heavy going to the modern eye and ear.

There's a tendency for beginner writers to have their characters constantly using each other's name in a conversation:

'I know, Josh, it's awful.'

'Yes, indeed, Mary, I don't know what to say.'

'But, Josh, we must do something!'

'I guess so, maybe we could stop referring to each other by name, since we know that already – and besides, there's nobody else in the room?'

'What a good idea, Josh!'

So, if it's obvious that it's only Josh and Mary speaking, dispense with the verbal reference – or indicate by gestures linked to the character's words, e.g.:

Josh ran a hand over his face. 'I'm really worried.'

Mary's eyes searched his face. 'What about?'

Try to convey the period, the person's profession and background, and the character with the use of appropriate vocabulary.

Dialogue can also suggest mood or emotion in a scene. A shared painful past is hinted at in the pages of *The $300 Man*, where Corbin meets Jean (pp. 18–22). It's a rather lengthy sample, but I think it illustrates many of the points already discussed. Here, I've tried to underplay the anguish and create a mood through dialogue, gesture and observation. Yes, dialogue isn't always in speech – but in body language.

He rapped on the door with his hook.

'Who is it?' Jeannie's voice was throaty and tremulous; perhaps a little rougher round the edges than he remembered.

'It's the man who saved you from Turner's knife.'

'Yes, of course, Mrs Begley said you'd be back.'

The key in the lock turned.

He thought it odd that she should lock the door now though not while she was being intimate with her customers.

He heard her move away from the door and some wooden furniture creaked. 'Come in,' she said.

Opening the door, he tried to smother the memory from an hour earlier, when Jeannie had been threatened and bleeding. He entered the room, taking off his hat, and closed the door after him.

She sat in a rocking chair. Looking at him from hollowed eye sockets, she seemed malnourished. The jutting cones of her breasts were more pronounced than he recalled, pressing against some white gauzy material while her legs were covered by a white frilly petticoat. Her feet were bare. She hadn't managed to clean away all the blood, he noticed; there were traces on the bridge of her left foot.

'Thank you for stopping Mr Turner, sir,' she said, and offered a lopsided smile.

Her smile hadn't been that way before, he realised. Something had altered her face – her nose still turned up at the tip, but it had been broken and was now slightly askew. The freckles were barely noticeable under the powder. Her thin lips usually offered the promise of a winsome smile but now they were dark red and unnatural. At one time her hazel eyes sent his heart soaring when she looked at him, but now she was hardly focussing on him or her world. Her mind was in some dark and distant place. Life once brimmed from her, now it was little more than a flickering candle in a gale.

'Have your cuts been doctored?'

She blinked, returning from her reverie, and nodded. 'Mrs Begley brought in Doc Bassett. He sewed up two cuts and the rest weren't too deep. The iodine stings, but he says I'll be OK.'

'Just keep the wounds clean,' he said. He refrained from commenting on how many young lives he'd witnessed being snuffed out on account of dirty wounds.

'Thank you for caring, Mister.' Her smile was thin, fragile, as if she was afraid that it may be misconstrued, his kindness sullied.

Hands gripping the brim of his hat, he said, 'You don't recognise me, Jean, do you?'

'No, I can't say as I do.' She gave him another travesty of a smile. 'You appreciate, I entertain many gentlemen. Unfortunately, my memory isn't as good as it was, you know?' She lowered her feet to the floorboards and thrust herself out of the chair, which creaked in protest at being abandoned.

'Let me take a good look at you,' she said, gliding up to him. She still walked with an enchanting serene movement; once, he'd thought of her as poetry in motion.

He looked down at her and he could see the stirrings of memory reasserting something in her, in the glinting of her eyes.

Brow wrinkled, she glanced at his hook and then his skewed nose. 'We make a good pair, don't we?' she said.

'Yes, I guess we do.'

She eyed the small scar on his forehead. Reaching up, she brushed a hand gently through his black hair, lingering on the clump of white hair on the left, just above the scar. At one time her touch would have sent his heart pounding; now he just felt sad. Finally, her gaze lingered on his. There was no mistake. Recognition widened her eyes and moisture formed at the rims. She stepped back a pace, a hand rising to her chest, over her heart. What little colour she had seemed to drain from her face. 'Corbin? Is it really you?'

'Yes.'

'Oh, my God,' she whispered, turning away. She crossed over to the bed and sat down, studying her feet and let tears fall to the floor where they darkened the dust and wood. 'Oh, my God.' A small fist beat at her right breast, plaintively.

He moved to sit beside her on the bed but refrained from touching her. 'It's been a long time, Jean.'

She nodded. 'A lifetime.'

Having observed the change wrought in her, he could understand how she must feel. He'd last seen her in '62 – twelve years ago.

'You've changed,' she said, her hands resting in her lap. Turning her head, she studied him, eyes ranging over his broad shoulders and muscular arms and thighs. 'You're taller, bigger – quite a man now, Corbin.' She shook her head. 'I didn't know about the hand – well, anything really.'

He could feel the trembling of her body transmitted through the bed's mattress. At any other time he might have appreciated the irony, of sitting here on a bed with her; in those far-off days he had coveted her young nubile form, though he hadn't rightly understood all the emotions that had threshed through his adolescent frame. Now, he understood all too well.

Gently, he placed his hand on hers. 'Life changes us. I've

been through a war – and a lot besides.'

She gave a wan smile. 'You don't want to know what I've endured, Corbin. You really don't.' She looked away again, the back of her hand wiping the tears from mottled cheeks. 'Best you just go and leave me be.'

Corbin shook his head. 'No, I came to see you. I'm not leaving.'

She faced him again, her eyes wide with a cynical edge to them, which he found surprisingly distasteful. Her upper lip curled. 'You want me, is that it?'

'No, Jean. I didn't turn up here as a customer.'

'Client,' she corrected.

'Whatever. As it happens, you're the fourth Jean I've tracked down. The others were false trails.'

'Tracked down?'

'Oh, I haven't made it my business. Sometimes, though, in my travels, I get to hear about a woman called Jean and the description seems to fit yours.' He eyed her copper-coloured hair and felt impelled to stroke it, as if that motion would brush away the past so they could return to those times of innocence. He raised a hand and gestured vaguely. 'So I take a detour, just to put my mind at rest. Today, my detour found the real Jean.'

'But why are you looking for me?' Her eyes shone with a forlorn hope.

'I wanted to be sure that you're all right. And there are a few things I need to know – things only you can tell me.'

Attribution

First of all, so long as it's clear who is speaking – either from the actual speech or from a prefatory reference to the character's physical action – there is no need for anything, not even the simple 'he said' tag.

If you must use the attribution, then place 'he said' in different places – in the middle of a speech, after the first sentence, perhaps. I want my readers to know who is speaking as soon as possible, so they can *see* that character speaking. It doesn't help the reader to read six lines of dialogue that then ends with 'John said.' It should be obvious as early as possible that it's John speaking.

In the example above, I've avoided attribution as much as possible:

'Who is it?' Jeannie's voice was throaty and tremulous...

The attribution is in the description of the speaker's (Jeannie's) voice.

Again, further down, I use description to introduce a character's speech:

She blinked, returning from her reverie, and nodded. 'Mrs Begley brought in Doc Bassett...'

It's obvious that it's Jeannie speaking; I don't have to labour the point. There are only two people in the room, so it should be clear who is speaking most of the time, without any specific attribution.

Occasionally, I relent:

'Oh, my God,' she whispered, turning away.

Because here I'm indicating a tone and an emotional reaction in response to Corbin's presence, I've inserted the 'whispered' tag.

Remember, this scene is from Corbin's POV, so any emotional turmoil that Jeannie's undergoing has to be conveyed in her facial expression, gestures, tone of voice and her words. For example, her simple short heartfelt response, 'A lifetime,' tells us that she feels buffeted by the years.

Harking back to the flippant Josh and Mary scenario above, you can see also that these two characters – Corbin and Jean – don't constantly use each other's name; she uses 'Corbin' three times, that's all. He uses 'Jean' six times, but three of those are to explain his search, tracking down other women with her name.

Alternatives

You're probably aware of the hundreds of synonyms for 'said', such as, 'I'm not sure,' the sheriff demurred.

While it depends on the type of story you're writing, it's usually the case that the majority of these synonyms should not be used. Stick to the simple variant, 'he said', 'she said', 'said Jake' and let the actions and spoken words convey the emotion and meaning.

Indeed, there are hundreds of alternatives to 'he said' to be found in Roget's Thesaurus, if you look hard enough, but you'd be well advised to use them sparingly – indeed, only when the synonym helps to characterize the speaker. I know of a few writing guides that list them – though to what effect, I'm not sure.

For some odd reason, the majority of readers barely register 'he said' – it's almost invisible – but are brought up short with those alternatives and thus they're no longer lost in the story.

There's a tendency for modern western and crime writers to overdo the use of 'he said', as if they're making a point. Yet for most instances, even the majority of the times that 'he said' is used, it isn't necessary.

I've lost count of the number of times I've read something like, 'Do as you're told, Mayor!' he hissed.

To hiss is to make a sibilant sound, like a snake, which requires the speech to have some esses in it. Science fiction writer Kenneth Bulmer pointed this out to me thirty-odd years ago. What is usually meant is that the character *whispered harshly or sternly.*

Another example is, 'I'm sure the lynching'll go without any problem,' he smiled. Ever tried smiling while speaking? There should be a full stop at the end of the speech and 'He smiled' capitalized.

When people speak, they're not always grammatically correct, and use word contractions, such as *I've* and *haven't* and *I'll* and *can't*. Your characters should too. Speech without contractions is invariably unrealistic.

Lengthy speech

You'll see it in published books, but it doesn't mean it's right. I'm talking about the lengthy speech a character makes. There are a few times when you can get away with a half-page of speech by a single character:

- The character is giving a lecture.
- The character is quoting from a book, perhaps...
- The character is prone to this verbal diarrhoea, tedious though it is.
- The character is delivering a monologue and nobody is present, perhaps...

As you can see, the last two instances are stretching it a bit!

Outside a lecture hall, in real-life dialogue, it's rare for a single person to speak unbrokenly, uninterruptedly for any length of time. There'll be interjections, alternative viewpoints postulated and hand gestures and facial expressions. People don't speak grammatically – and often their sentences are short.

If your character speaks for over six lines of dialogue, then it's probably not realistic, and therefore suspect. Break it up with the character's facial expression, appropriate hand gestures and body language, and with interruptions from the others present, even it it's just a question.

In the example above, I broke up Corbin's speech thus:

'Oh, I haven't made it my business. Sometimes, though, in my travels, I get to hear about a woman called Jean and the description seems to fit yours.' He eyed her copper-coloured hair and felt impelled to stroke it, as if that motion would brush away the past so they could return to those times of innocence. He raised a hand and gestured vaguely. 'So I take a detour, just to put my mind at rest. Today, my detour found the real Jean.'

I could just have used his speech, and that would have taken up only four lines of dialogue. But by adding Corbin's stillborn gesture, I broke up even those four lines – and added imagery and emotion.

Inevitably, there are times when I break the six lines of dialogue rule. On p. 95, Major Newton delivers seven and a half lines of speech, but it's a rarity in the book, and serves to characterise the major. Know the rules – and when to break them.

Other niggles

Avoid the too frequent use of the introductory "Well,...' And if a character does use it, then ensure that he alone does, not everyone.

Dash it. You can use a dash in dialogue

- To indicate an abrupt break in a sentence – perhaps when the speaker is interrupted
- In place of brackets when using a parenthesis – it somehow reads smoother
- To precede an afterthought – at the end of a sentence
- To emphasize – a dramatic pause – in a speech
- To show when a speech is broken by strong emotion, or hesitancy, or nerves, or stammering –

Some writing guides and agents advocate 'start a new speech on a new line/paragraph.' This has been taken to nonsensical extremes. I've seen writers abide by this so that they've separated all speech from any associated character gesture or expression. The main objective is to show the reader who is speaking at all times – so they can see it in their mind's eye. The rule for dialogue is: one speaker, one paragraph (and that includes narrative relating to the speaker).

Laughed used instead of 'he said'. This is quite annoying – and used by published authors, to their shame. It's no joke.

'We robbed a bank,' he laughed.

Have you tried to speak and laugh at the same time? Barely possible. The other variation is 'he smiled', which I've already touched on, and is just as absurd.

Fine, you can write: 'We robbed a bank.' He laughed.

That didn't hurt, did it? And at least it's right.

Weather reports. You've probably read a published novel that begins with a first paragraph about the weather. Maybe it creates a great mood and even a sense of place. But it has no purpose in a western genre novel. You need to begin your book with action or, at the very least, conflict.

Listen to your characters

As you move on through the writing process of your novel, you might hear your characters talking, interacting. This is not the time to send for the men in white coats – it's a time to rejoice, because you've invested them with sufficient reality so that they *seem* real in your mind.

You're eavesdropping in on their conversations.

If this occurs, jot down in your plot-plan what you 'hear'. It may be raw, but it might well be real for that character, so you can use it. Obviously, this happens the more you immerse yourself in your characters and their world, the world you've created.

11

Description and Visualization

Narrative and observational description are necessary to create mood, a sense of place and to deepen a reader's knowledge of the characters. To be used sparingly, judiciously, even, and only through the characters' eyes – unless you're opting for an omniscient POV, of course.

> Heaven's Gateway was an imposing edifice, its three storeys dwarfing the neighbouring shops and offices. Its entrance portico boasted granite pillars and steps, while the boardwalk that ran around the building was varnished teak. Drapes of a variety of red hues adorned the windows; balustraded balconies on the two upper floors were colourfully festooned with women wearing long silk dresses and low necklines.
>
> Having changed his clothes in the back of Ma Chong's, Corbin felt slightly better as he approached the bordello. A ginger-haired soiled dove leaned over the rail, a black cigarita in her hand. She called out, 'Hey, Mister, ask for Ginger – I can give you a good time – all night for $30.'
>
> He paused and removed his black slouch hat. 'Thanks kindly, ma'am, but I've a prior booking.' He climbed the steps and, standing in the shade of the balcony, he pulled the bell.
>
> He heard Ginger swear. 'Since when did Ma Begley take bookings?
>
> (*The $300 Man*, p. 14)

Narrative description

Some writers feel more comfortable writing narrative description and less so with dialogue. A book filled with narrative description will be a slow read, tending to appear stodgy, with little 'white space' on the page; indeed, quite daunting to some readers.

Dialogue breaks up the page, makes it easier on the eye.

So resist the temptation to write swathes of unbroken description.

Whatever scene setting you write, it should be through a character's eyes.

Setting the scene

A novel is a sequence of dramatic points. There's no magic number of dramatic points, however. Each dramatic scene should move the story forward and present conflict for one or more characters.

Soddy Station comprised a long sod house with four rooms, one of which was usually set aside for female stagecoach travellers. There was the station master, his wife and the hostler. The main room held a long trestle table with three legged stools arranged around it. The walls had been papered with pictures from 'A journal of civilization', *Harper's Weekly* and the pages from a general store catalogue. A number of spittoons lined one wall.

Corbin thought that the food was passable for a dollar a head: hot biscuits and antelope steaks.

Javier Jara didn't seem to like it much, hardly touching the steak. 'A little overdone for my taste,' he whispered to Corbin when the hefty station mistress was in the kitchen.

'I reckon the master's ex-cowboy – they like their steaks well done.'

'Sacrilege, I tell you! I want to taste the flesh and its juices, not charcoal.'

Corbin smiled in agreement then shrugged. He'd long ago learned to eat whatever was available and be glad of it. Food in the belly meant strength in the body, which might be useful in an unexpected and dire situation. (p. 66)

So, here we're given a visual of the staging station, but also we get to experience the new friendship between Javier and Corbin, important for later in the story. So the description is leavened with a bit of characterisation and broken up with dialogue – and food!

Some writers say that if a scene has no conflict in it, then jettison it. Alternatively, find some conflict in that scene. Above, the minor conflict is Javier's dislike of overcooked steak. Cowboys preferred their steaks well done.

If a town or village figures prominently in your narrative, then sketch the position of the houses, shops, hotels, pubs etc. so when Jim leaves the hotel and turns right, you know where he's heading. Because otherwise next time he leaves, he might turn right but end up somewhere else and somewhere quite illogical!

Don't be reluctant to sketch a plan of a room in a scene, so you know where individuals are standing. If a fight is going to take place in the room, then you need to know the whereabouts of the obstacles, potential weapons, furniture and people, so make that sketch.

For example, on p. 81 – 'The town's two hotels were on opposite sides of the main street. Corbin left the stage depot and carried his bags up the wide steps...'

Early on, I'd drawn a map of the town and named the shops, saloons etc. If the storyline veered somewhere I hadn't bargained for, then that 'somewhere else' was inserted on the map for future reference.

Map of Walkerville

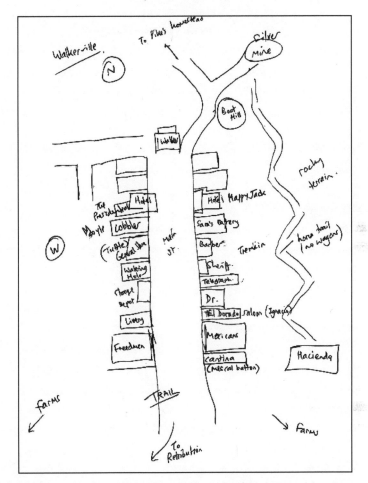

This is the map I used while writing The $300 Man. I have a more detailed map of Bethesda Falls, as that's become a town I return to for different adventures, involving various characters – whether barbers, barkeeps, the mayor or the sheriff.

Visualization

Remember, a book is a movie inside a reader's head. Setting the scene means seeing it in your mind's eye. This might entail zooming in on details or even panning around a street scene, particularly when you're writing in omniscient mode.

Visualization is often neglected, especially in a first draft. If you can't 'see' it, then your readers most certainly can't.

People don't exist in a vacuum – they're standing, sitting, lounging, and walking in a solid world of your making. Let the readers see it – but let them see *through your characters' eyes.*

This applies for every scene, to varying degrees, depending on the importance of the dramatic incident.

Use all the senses when possible – sight, touch, smell, sound and taste.

'Well, come in.' She stood aside, swept the slight train of her dress behind her and gestured for him to enter the hallway. She shut the door. 'You've come to the right place, to be sure. Hang your hat, Mister.'

He hung the slouch on a mahogany hook by the door.

Turning on her heel with a swishing sound of satin, she said, 'Follow me, sir.'

He did so, trailing behind her swaying red bustle as it swept over the narrow strip of hall carpet. Even though it was still day, wall sconces were lit, projecting a warm ruddy glow everywhere Corbin looked. There was a sickly-sweet smell of cheap perfume, which he surmised probably served to keep at bay the pungent aroma of body odour and tobacco smoke. He heard murmuring up ahead.

Once he had passed through an arched doorway, a heavy brocade curtain fell behind him and all sound ceased. They were in a large room, each wall lined with two or three chaise longues, the walls papered in a crimson flock design. Seats were either occupied by young women with painted faces or anxious-looking men of all ages. The women wore white dimity wide skirts and soft ringlets of hair cascaded over bare shoulders; some fluttered lace fans in front of dark coquettish eyes. Most of the men only gave him a cursory look then returned to studying their boots or chatting to each other; the women too resumed their conversation, ignoring him. It was as if they were all congregated in a railway station waiting room. Only here the tickets were to Paradise, even if it was ephemeral. (p. 15)

You need to personalise the visualization, too. Using the earlier sequence where Corbin meets Jean after many years, I'll give an example:

Her smile hadn't been that way before, he realised. Something had altered her face – her nose still turned up at the tip, but it had been broken and was now slightly askew. The freckles were barely noticeable under the powder. Her thin lips usually offered the promise of a winsome smile but now they were dark red and unnatural. At one time her hazel eyes sent his heart soaring when she looked at him, but now she was hardly focussing on him or her world. Her mind was in some dark and distant place. Life once brimmed from her, now it was little more than a flickering candle in a gale.

She'd offered him a lopsided smile, which set off his memory of a younger, more innocent Jean. We see how she is now and how she was, in stark contrast. It's visual description, but combined with Corbin's emotion-filled memories and the maturity he'd gained since last seeing her.

Show, don't tell

Because people are used to seeing films, where it's all visual and the story isn't told from a character's perspective, new writers tend to write what happens and to whom, but there's no actual POV. It's all 'tell': *Joe went here, Alice said this, and it was dark…*

There are sections in any book where it's convenient or necessary to simply tell the reader what's going on, rather than show it. Sometimes, simply showing can slow down the story. But keep these instances to a minimum.

On p. 26, I *tell* some of Jean's story. It's tell almost all the way, but interspersed with the odd phrase of dialogue to show it's her telling Corbin, not the reader.

Here's an example of telling and showing. If I wanted simply to tell, I could have written:

Corbin left the stage depot and went into the Happy Jack Hotel. The desk clerk took his bags.

The scene and the action hardly register. Instead, I wrote:

Corbin left the stage depot and carried his bags up the wide steps and under the portico of the Happy Jack Hotel. Opening the tall glass-paned door, he entered to the accompaniment of a jangling bell. A young man in a dark blue outfit hurried across the carpeted foyer to relieve Corbin of his bags. He faltered only a second on noting the hook. (p. 81)

Now, we have a sense of the scene – and also see how others perceive Corbin.

Here's another example, from the POV of a villain, Mort (p. 31):

Smoke spiralled up from the Winchesters of the six gunmen who surrounded the homestead. The night was filled with the after-echo from several hundred rounds of ammunition being fired. It was dark but out here the starlight and the moon's glow provided sufficient visibility, though Mort reckoned the shadows were threatening. Since he was a kid, he'd feared shadows. Maybe since his pa came at him so often out of that darkness. He wiped the sweat of memories away and leaned forward in his saddle, hands on the pommel. He tasted the gun smoke and spat on the ground. He could see the roofed portico, its pillars pitted with bullet-holes; the two wooden chairs and the small three-legged table barely resembled their original shape, so many shells had peppered into them. The bullet-riddled front door was slightly ajar and a white flag was wafting up and down on the end of a Henry repeater rifle.

It almost appears as if the viewpoint is omniscient – and, often, western writers jump that way in similar scenes. But by injecting 'though Mort reckoned…' I'm personalising it as his viewpoint. So the rest of the scene will be visualised from his POV. The intention was to let the reader, through Mort's senses, see the state of the building – the roofed portico, its pillars pitted with bullet holes etc.

You can see that it's dark, but stars and the moon provide sufficient visibility.

Always beware of night scenes – how does the protagonist see what's going on; where's the source of light?

I would like to think that you can also virtually taste the gun smoke, and hear the after-echo of the shots, the saddle leather creaking. Some of these small but significant details were inserted at the layering stage, mentioned in the next chapter.

And if nothing else then good writing is meant to evoke sensation in the reader – as one writer put it, 'not the fact that it's raining, but the feeling of being rained upon.'

Flora and fauna

A western novel isn't just about the characters – it's about the land. A land that is rich in variety. Indeed, in some westerns the land can almost become a 'character'. It certainly provides conflict.

So, don't neglect the flora and fauna. Of course, since you've set a time period for your western – say, July 1879 – then you can research for plants that flower in July. If you stick to a vague time period, you're hampered and are liable to mix and match and maybe get nature's calendar cockeyed.

He [Corbin] ducked under the lintel, shut the door behind him and breathed in the fresh night air.

Crickets chirruped, invisible and insistent, and thousands of stars winked in the black sky. Over to the right an array of cactus plants resembled men approaching in surrender, arms held high.

Fortunately, the wind was to the west so he didn't get the smell from the stables. He chided himself for being uncharitable; maybe they didn't muck out as often as they should, but these station masters did very well by their horses. Resting and feeding them and being ready at a moment's notice to replace an unexpected team. What must it have been like when this territory was still prey to raids by warriors on the warpath? Lonely and very isolated, even if the next station was only about ten miles off. Stagecoaches pulling in, pierced by arrows and more resembling porcupines than modes of transport; and then those stages that had never arrived, their carcasses littering the prairie. He withdrew his hat, transferred it to his double hook and wiped the inner brim with the heel of his right hand. (pp. 67/68)

Nothing unusual, maybe, just crickets, stars and cactus, but hopefully it conveys the vastness of the prairie and the stillness – just before a provoking incident occurs.

In another western, I injected some natural imagery:

As their journey progressed through tall grasses interspersed with blue-white beardtongue, he found that he was again deeply stirred by her. She rode easy in the saddle and was a competent horsewoman. She was really knowledgeable about nature too, pointing out where he was likely to catch bobwhite quail and ring-necked pheasant. Her enthusiasm was infectious. 'You should be here in the Spring,' she told him. 'The meadows east of the town are a purple blaze of Pasqueflower.'

The woman is a schoolteacher and keen about geography, and enthuses her young students. This scene is the calm before a fresh onslaught threatens their lives and binds the pair closer.

Weather Lore

No, you don't have to be a weatherman. But, like the landscape of the Old West, the weather can become an antagonist in the western novel. At the very least, you should be aware of the weather your characters are living through.

Is it always sunny? Or are there rainy days. Both the sun and rain can provide drama and incident so don't neglect them. In my novel *Old Guns*, the present action took place in July 1892, which was the hottest period for seventeen years, and people expired from the heat.

As one cowboy remarked about a hot July day, 'It makes you feel as if you'd washed yourself in molasses and water.' A great slice of imagery!

12

Symbolism and Layering

Some people have the misguided idea that you'll only find symbolism in 'literary' fiction. Not so. Symbols – any physical object or phrase, gesture, animal – can augment your theme. One literary definition of a symbol is 'a person, event or thing that stands for or represents by association some other, usually broader, idea or range of ideas, in addition to maintaining its own literal meaning.'

A symbol provides that little extra depth in your book. While it's probably there already in your story, it sometimes needs a nudge for emphasis. That nudge often comes during the layering process.

By layering, I mean returning to scenes written earlier and inserting additional information – whether physical description, extra backstory, more emotional content or more profound internal dialogue. It can be done piecemeal, as you write, jumping to and fro in the story as ideas surface and re-echo. It can be done towards the end, before the self-edit stage.

Symbolism

The most effective method for injecting a symbol is by evoking its recurrence. Some writers consider that symbols are theatrical and obvious, but they don't have to be either. Often, they're not noticed by the reader, save at a second reading. A reader who discerns these symbols – when they aren't too obvious – connects that little bit more with your story.

Don't strive to insert symbols that appear out of place. They have to be natural for the story, or they'll simply jar or seem pretentious.

The hook worn by Corbin Molina is significant. It serves as a deadly weapon and saves him more than once. He's not less of a man, but more of a man with it.

The title of the Prologue is 'The Hook', which in filmic terms means, the hook to pull the reader in, which it tends to do. And the symbolism runs full circle to the Epilogue, entitled 'El Gancho', which is Spanish for 'the hook', a nickname the Mexicans have given Molina. And of course Malinda plays on the words, to state that she's hooked – in love.

The hook has its part to play in several scenes. But it's also simply there – 'He rapped on the door with his hook.' (p 18)

Poetry is often about love and loss, and it's loaded with symbolism. A book of Walt Whitman's poems saved Corbin's life. Poetry is also important to Dr Malinda Dix.

> As she gently placed the book in his good hand, Corbin noticed that she had a strawberry birthmark on her left temple. His fingers traced the deep gouge in the cover of *Leaves of Grass*.
>
> 'This chunk of shrapnel was dug out of your book, Captain,' she said, retrieving the shard from a metal dish. 'Fortunately, you kept the book over your heart.' (p. 107)

The symbolism relates to his heart, which he loses to her, and as the scene changes to many years later, he feels his heart pounding as he opens the doctor's surgery door.

Layering

While it's obvious that the book's a western – its cover and blurb tell us as much – it isn't always clear when the action occurs. So, for example, in the first paragraph of Chapter One, I insert an oblique reference to the date of the current events:

> Banners strung across the main street announced that in a week's time Retribution would be celebrating its twenty-first

year since its founding day way back on July 19, 1853. Corbin wasn't in any mood for rejoicing: he'd killed two men. (p. 11)

– twenty-one years after 1853. Indeed, that fact was layered in afterwards, during a rewriting stage.

This layering is done as you gain more insight into the characters on their journey; you realize you need to slot in some facts earlier, or insert a few red herrings, maybe; or provide some foreshadowing. It most definitely is not padding. It's there to deepen the reader's experience, enrich the imagery and better define the characters, the scene and the mood.

As you return to rewrite and self-edit, you'll be tempted to add additional dialogue, description and emotion. This is fine, so long as it isn't repetition and adds depth in some way. Don't add words for the sake of building up that word count. Each revisit to a scene might entail inserting an additional layer – even if only a few *significant* words.

Foreshadowing

This means laying the groundwork for what is to come. If the hero is going to brain the villain with a wooden chair, it pays to mention the existence of that chair earlier on. If the heroine is going to evade the attacker with her Derringer, then the reader should be aware of the gun's existence before this.

Subtler foreshadowing drops hints about a character's behaviour that materialise later in a dramatic moment.

There's a particular type of author intrusive foreshadowing, which goes along the lines of this example:

Unknown to Baker, he was being hunted on that cold Montana evening. He had been seen by Coyote Breath and two Sioux warriors. The Indians were slipping up on him while the young white man washed his plate and eating irons in the creek.

Whose viewpoint is this? The author's – maybe omniscient, at a pinch. But it's foreshadowing that the Sioux hunters are going to catch up with Baker. I'd rather the reader found out about the hunters catching up with Baker at the actual event, without any foreshadowing narrative. And of course referring to Baker as 'the young white man' jerks the reader out of any pretence of being in Baker's POV,

So, don't tell us what is about to happen, just show us when it happens.

Story tempo

Your story shouldn't flow in a flat simple manner, its tone level. There should be ups and downs, peaks and troughs, with a fast and a slow pace, depending on the dramatic scene and the emotion invested in the characters.

Some authors deliberately draw a timeline for their story and chapters and then insert points where the highs will appear – usually towards the end of chapters/major scenes – and they also indicate the lows.

If the story is a constant pell-mell rush to the finish, the reader can hardly stop for breath. Moments of reflection are therefore welcome; though keep them brief as a western is essentially an action story. The danger is in making those reflective moments too slow – and therefore reducing the reader's urge to turn the page. So, even those quiet phases have to contain some kind of conflict, dilemma or obstacle – mental or physical.

Fast narrative needs short crisp sentences, perhaps with dialogue. Use active prose.

Slower-paced narrative can be more leisurely and the dialogue doesn't have to be as succinct or as urgent. And, up to a point, you can adopt more passive prose.

13

Beginnings and Endings

It seems obvious, but beginnings and endings are very important. But don't fret over them too much – at least until the book is written. Then you can decide how you want to shape the beginning and the ending.

Mickey Spillane said, 'The beginning sells this book, the ending sells the next book.'

The ending mustn't be rushed but it shouldn't linger longer than necessary.

It's understandable, you've lived with these characters for the time it takes to write the novel and there's a natural reluctance to leave them. Resist the urge to delay leaving. End the novel as soon as you can, making sure that it's a satisfying conclusion.

Opening and closing scenes

A phrase from scriptwriting is helpful: begin late, leave early. In other words, enter a scene as late as possible, at the crucial plot point; and once something is resolved, don't hang around, get out of that scene.

At the start of each chapter and scene, I attempt to avoid 'It' and 'The'. Not always successfully – in *The $300 Man*, they occur on pp. 34, 37, 71, 76, 112, 115, 138, 143 – which isn't bad, considering the number of scene changes and fourteen chapters.

Scene changes are useful to avoid having to show your characters going from A to B. Close scene at A. Start the next one at B.

On p. 37 I have the last words: 'I have business to attend to in Walkerville.'

The next scene is in Walkerville, though through the eyes of someone else.

This kind of scene-change employs a cinematic device, an echo effect. Walkerville is the last word of the previous scene and it's in the first line of the new scene. This isn't unconscious repetition but a deliberate echo.

And on p. 45, at the end of a scene, the sheriff says, 'That Jeremiah doesn't know how close he came to knocking on the gates of hell.'

While the start of the next scene shows us 'Jeremiah sat nursing the mug of coffee...' The link from one scene to the next is Jeremiah.

Scene changes are useful for conveying memories or flashback scenes. I employ flashback scenes in this novel to provide backstory, increase emotional involvement and to create more depth of character.

'I wanted to be sure that you're all right. And there are a few things I need to know – things only you can tell me.'

Strange, how some memories had sustained him through the fighting. Then, afterwards, when he learned the truth, he tried so hard to deny those self-same memories. Yet, despite the heartache, they were his past, part of the fabric that made him what he was, who he was. (p 22)

So, the scene ends with Corbin wanting to know some things that only Jean can tell him. Then the scene shifts – or glides – into his memories of twelve years ago.

You're more likely to insert specific scene changes to echo an action or thing during the layering or self-edit phase. As mentioned, this echoing is used frequently in films. Some aspect at the endpoint of a film scene is repeated or inverted or echoed in the start point of the new scene – whether a door closing in one scene and then another door opening in the next, or a sound or dialogue phrase is repeated.

So, for example at the end of Chapter 4 (p. 60) Sheriff Deshler says, 'The town can pay.' And at the start of Chapter 5 (p. 61) Sheriff Clegg drops five dollars from his pay.

Another instance of an echo, this time about emotion:

She swallowed, surprised at her own diagnosis: she was quite lonely and rather sad.

The sad procession drove into Walkerville late afternoon. Corbin pulled in the wagon outside the sheriff's office. The shingle gave the lawman's name: Avery Clegg. Tying up the horses by a water-trough, he mounted the wooden steps to the boardwalk. (p. 76)

The doctor reflects on her self-diagnosis – quite lonely and rather *sad*. And in the next scene, 'The *sad* procession drove into Walkerville.' This repetition is deliberate, to maintain and strengthen the sombre mood.

Try not to make these echoes appear contrived. Not every scene change lends itself to this treatment – so leave well alone if that's the case, rather than strive for an awkward effect.

14

Self-edit

In this day of authors creating their own e-books, it's important to understand that the self-edit stage is crucial and sadly frequently neglected. A good story can be spoiled for the reader if it's poorly edited.

I don't mean the inevitable few typos that sneak in despite the best efforts of author, editor and proofreader, but rather the careless and many errors that signify that scant care has been taken in the final editing check; indeed, on occasion, one suspects there was no final editing check at all!

Spellcheck

Worse, sometimes, I've received manuscript submissions where it's clear the author hasn't used a spellchecker – the red-under-lined words jump out.

Yes, you have to be wary of the spellchecker, it isn't always accurate – for some reason mine gets *its* and *it's* mixed up, and *they're* and *their*.

And you can't simply rely on the spellchecker to be your attempt at self-edit. The spellchecker won't detect the wrong word: say, complement instead of compliment.

Mistakes happen

This may sound like heresy, but no book is perfect, no matter how much time the author and editors spend on it. Henry James continually amended his published novels, much to his publisher's annoyance. Modern best-selling authors are perhaps the worst culprits. Danielle Steel's rather good book *The Ring* has no less than 52 typographical errors in it, but it has been reprinted many times and hasn't suffered in sales. The American classic *To Kill a Mockingbird* – my copy (1997) shows it has been reprinted 42 times – has a glaring error on the first page – '*Out* father said we were both right' – instead of '*Our* father said we were both right.' A fellow author's hardback was irretrievably published with a blurb that stated 1989 when it should have been 1889!

A while back, I invented the Editor's Curse: *the reader spots the things I missed but doesn't see all the good I've done.* An editor mustn't expect thanks, though they occur sometimes. We're simply guides; if we want praise for written work, we must write our own.

So, mistakes happen, no matter how hard we try to avoid them. But that's no reason to be cavalier about self-editing, proof-reading and final checks.

Before sending the book to a publisher, the writer needs to take a step back from the work and read it clinically. A book is never finished, it's abandoned – but don't abandon it too soon!

Don't rush it

Or you might misplace a few hundred people... I'm speaking from experience, honest. Some years ago, I sent off to the publisher my finished western novel. It was accepted and duly went through the editing process and eventually I checked the galleys, advising of a few minor things.

Only when a reader purchased the printed book did my error come to light. At the outset of the story, I'd stipulated the population of the town on a welcome sign. And at the end of the book, I did the same, minus a few killed by the hero. Unfortunately, at some point in the rewriting phase I'd decided to increase the population of the town by three hundred – and amended the town notice at the beginning of the book. But I must have been sidetracked – phone call or whatever – in the process and neglected to reflect that change at the end of the book. So in effect I lost three hundred folk from that town – maybe the aliens took them! I owned up to the publisher, but it was too late by then, the book was in print.

Undaunted, I got round that error when writing another western set in the same town. The signwriter got the sack for messing up the numbers and never lived it down...

The moral – if you change something, make doubly sure that your change doesn't have to be reflected elsewhere in the book. Do that vital word-search, at the very least!

Editing as a blood sport

[A similar version to this section was published in *Writing Magazine* a few years ago under my by-line. I've included it, suitably tweaked, as I believe it is pertinent and may provide additional insight for that final self-edit phase.]

Publishers need editors because, heretical thought, books are not necessarily acquired for their literary quality but perhaps for their story content and their subjects' commercial appeal.

If your book has been accepted, the process can be a great deal faster and the book can be published much earlier if only light editing is required. For that reason, I would make a strong plea to all writers: the final author self-edit is *vital*.

To achieve that final edit, step back from your work and appraise it with fresh eyes. Never send off a manuscript unless this final read-through has been done with a critical eye. As a commissioning editor I've rejected many manuscripts because it was obvious that this final reread wasn't performed.

In the old days, an editor and author might have worked on the book together physically. This is no longer necessary. Many, like me, work on the screen and communicate via e-mail and attachments. That remoteness is only in spatial terms, not in the relationship between author and editor.

Naturally, an author is very close to her creation. It may have taken many months or even years to get to this stage. It is a cliché, but some authors liken their books to their 'babies' and can be very defensive. That's quite understandable.

Editors are there to spot the inconsistent, the illogical and the incorrect items that the author couldn't identify because he was too close to the work. The author knows what he means, but is it clear to the reader? Are the events and actions depicted in a logical way? An editor is always striving for clarity of understanding.

I begin the working relationship with an author by proposing changes. The emphasis is on the 'proposing'. I'm not in the business of insisting on rewriting the book to suit my sensibilities. In the final analysis, it's the author's book, not mine. An editor strives to make the author look good by improving the book's appeal and narrative flow. Good writers appreciate intelligent editing; sadly, bad writers don't like being edited.

'Do no harm' is the editor's credo. Harm is done by altering the author's style or the meaning of the prose. A few writers might believe that editing is a blood sport and it's their baby being hunted. To retain the blood analogy, editing can be the fine line between surgery and butchery.

My editing is usually done in red on the electronic copy. I accompany the changes with a separate commentary sheet, explaining my reasoning. Some insertions are self-explanatory. I'm looking for spelling and typographical errors, lax or inconsistent punctuation and grammatical errors. All of which should rarely appear, *if* the author has done an adequate final self-edit.

Every writer – me included – will unwittingly reuse a particular word more than once in close proximity; this is called the 'echo effect' because that word is simply echoing in the writer's head at that time. Elsewhere it may be a different word entirely. I will point out word repetition by underlining the culprits; I'll offer alternatives or I may leave it for the writer to seek a more suitable replacement.

Successive sentences or paragraphs beginning with the same phrase or word can be tedious and threaten narrative flow.

Again, they will be highlighted and I'll ask the writer to seek variations.

Generalisations in fiction are not helpful to the reader. The author's aim is to create imagery in the reader's head – not overly detailed, but enough to assist the reader in visualising the scene, character or situation. You can't do that with generalisations. Wherever possible, be specific. If you mention a dog, why not define its breed? If your hero rides a horse, allocate a type. If your heroine wears a dress, specify its design or at the very least its colour.

At times, a scene may be too hurried or inadequately conveyed; the author hasn't used all of the scene's potential and this may be pointed out, to improve the drama, to create atmosphere and enhance characterisation. This should have been caught at the layering stage.

Sometimes, there may be a need to point out where an excess of 'tell' has been allowed to survive to the detriment of 'show.' Naturally, it depends on the story's flow, whether to show or tell. If you're in a dramatic scene, it has more emotional impact if you show the scene through the eyes and heart of a character, rather than simply describing what is happening.

Good writers have a visual sense. They see what is going on in each scene, very much like a movie producer, and write down that scene so that the reader can see it too. I may from time to time highlight a section that would benefit from additional visual cues.

An editor will identify clichés and mixed metaphors and the writer is advised to find fresh ways of saying what is meant.

If the reader has to stop and think about the writing sense itself, then the writer isn't doing his job properly. The cliché phrase 'lost in a good book' means exactly that. Any time the reader is pulled out of the world of the book, the writing is not doing its job.

That brings us to the story flow. Chapters and time breaks are useful, as they provide points where the real world can intrude. Those are designed breaks, however. As an editor I don't want to falter over an inept description, an inconsistent logical issue or an impossible scene; that stumble pulls me out of the story and upsets the narrative flow.

Striving for good narrative flow also entails seeking an economy of words. I've encountered writers who say the same thing in three different ways in one paragraph. Ideally, say as much as you can with as few words as possible.

All writers should read widely. Naturally, they should read books within the genre with which they're familiar. That's what is meant by 'write what you know'; the phrase doesn't mean, 'write about your boring job in the office'. Editors too need to read and should have an interest in many subjects, as this broad knowledge can be essential for spotting inconsistencies and inaccuracies. I need to know enough about any given subject to raise questions that a book's potential readership might ask.

My library of books to assist me in editing is also useful for guiding me in my writing. They include *The Oxford Dictionary for Writers and Editors*, *The Good English Guide*, *Copyediting: A Practical Guide*, *Usage and Abusage*, *The Complete Plain Words*, Lynne Truss' *Eats, Shoots and Leaves*, *The Economist Pocket Style Book*, *The Times Guide to English Style and Usage*, the *Oxford Dictionary of Foreign Words and Phrases*, *Collins Thesaurus* (in dictionary form) and the *Shorter Oxford Dictionary*, as well as about a dozen specialist dictionaries.

Editing requires perseverance, but it's fun and really satisfying when you see an author's book hit the shelves. The odd acknowledgement is quite nice too.

Things to look for

Echo words. As explained in the foregoing section, I don't mean those intentional ones, notably at scene changes. But where the same word crops up repeatedly on the same page. It's as if it has lodged in the forebrain and insists on being used time and again. Most writers are surprised when they're pointed out.

Ellipses. Use these sparingly. Earlier in my career, I tended to use them a lot… I don't know why… Maybe I wanted to end each sentence on a thoughtful note…? In retrospect, it was tedious to read.

Change of tense. Most fiction is written in the past historic. But occasionally an author gets carried away and lives the action in the moment and slips into the present tense. Watch out for tense switching.

Time. Sometimes, a writer will start a chapter or paragraph with 'An hour later, …' Fine, if the POV character is known to carry a fob watch or is in the vicinity of the town clock tower. Otherwise, how can he measure time so accurately?

Temperature. Similar issue to time, really. The hero is crawling through the desert; the sun is beating down on him. It's 108 degrees Fahrenheit. Only if he carries a thermometer. Brit and European writers, whose temperature is now Celsius, should be aware that in the Old West it was usually measured in degrees Fahrenheit.

Active and passive voice. Typically, in a western, a book of action, you should eschew the passive voice in most instances.

Active. The sheriff punched him in the jaw.

Passive. He was punched in the jaw by the sheriff.

Paragraphs. The space between paragraphs allows the reader to take a mental pause, to absorb what has gone before. There are no rules about paragraphs. Gabriel García Márquez's novel *The Autumn of the Patriarch* (1975) only contains three paragraphs!

It is advocated that a single paragraph contains a single thought or idea or perhaps action. All the sentences within it are related to that thought or image.

Where action is involved, the paragraphs should be short, as this moves the story along faster.

Words and phrases that might annoy

Based on editing experience, a number of words and phrases to consider for review are given below.

Although it isn't against any writing rule, considered opinion is that narrative flow is improved by avoiding 'It' and 'The' at the beginning of chapters, as commented on in Chapter 13.

Novice writers tend to overuse the following words. One way to avoid this repetition is to do a word-search. You'll be surprised how often that word crops up. Here are a few commonly overused and often unnecessary words or phrases:

- Down
- Up
- Out
- Just – no problem with the word, but I find that it crops up several times in the same page. Just be wary.
- Began to – this is passive. He began to run – rather, he ran.

Amount. Applies to mass or bulk, not to number. 'A large amount of guns' is wrong; it should be 'a large number of guns'.

Effect and affect. Note the difference! (*Usage and Abusage: A Guide to Good English* will tell you.)

That – your sentences can get tied in knots with too many 'thats'. Most can be jettisoned. That's a fact.

Had – I've encountered many a severe case of 'haditis'. Is every instance of the pluperfect really really necessary? Once it's established that you're referring to the past, you don't have to pile on the hads. Before long, I cry I've had enough!

Could see – what's wrong with 'saw'? Sometimes 'could see' is fine, but remember that 'saw' is more immediate and reads faster, while 'could see' is more leisurely.

Could hear – try 'heard'… Same reason as 'could see', really.

Came/coming – a non-visual word. There are so many alternatives, depending on the situation. He came into the room – he strode, he walked, he rushed, he loped... All visual, where 'came' isn't.

Verb-ing. Yes, I know, there's no such word. 'Walking to the end of the town street, he adjusted his gun belt.' So, what we have here is someone who is adjusting his weapon's belt *all the way along the street*. It should read, however: 'He adjusted his gun belt and walked to the end of the street.' Be wary when you're writing about continuous action.

Things – a niggling unhelpful word, rarely to be used, except perhaps in dialogue. If someone 'picked up her things' – let us know *what* was picked up.

Suddenly – repeated often. In *The $300 Man* I've got the word 'suddenly' eight times. When editing, I've seen it that many times on a page!

He thought to himself. Delete 'to himself' – who else could he think to?

Hissed – snakes hiss. Already covered, but worth reiterating.

Misspeaks (i.e.: to/too/two, your/you're, their/there/they're, its/it's, whose/who's, hear/here, etc. I don't understand how these can arise. It should be obvious where to use their or they're or there. But they crop up with regularity.

Possessives. For indicating possession with singular names, use 's: that is, Tim's, Jane's.

For family names, only use an apostrophe: the Jones' farm. Though Jones's is acceptable these days, it looks awful!

Disjointed flow. Abrupt changes in narrative can pull the reader out of the story.

'He halted his horse outside the lawman's office. Sitting opposite the sheriff, he...'

Visually, we've leaped from the back of the horse on to a chair in the sheriff's office.

This could have been alleviated by:

'He halted his horse outside the lawman's office. He dismounted, strode inside and without a word sat opposite the sheriff.'

Or, more simply: 'He halted his horse outside the lawman's office. Seconds later, he was sitting opposite the sheriff.'

Sentence spacing. In the old days, when I learned to touch-type, I was taught to leave two spaces between sentences. This is no longer necessary: one space between sentences will do. It's no big deal, however, as a blanket change can sort it out.

Titles. Titles are capitalized only when preceding a name (President Jackson, Captain Smith) or when used in direct address ('Hello, Captain Smith.' and 'Yes, Captain.'). In all other uses, they're lowercase: (She smiled at the detective, or 'I told the president yes,' she said.). The no-caps rule also applies to endearments: it's 'darling,' not 'Darling'; 'baby', not 'Baby'.

I don't know how Mom would like that... This is where Mom is in place of a name, so it's capitalised. *I don't know how my mom would like that...* This isn't capitalized because it isn't specifying her by name (Mom).

Roaming eyes. Make sure sentences are clear: His eyes roamed the street – eyes don't roam. A gaze may roam, but not the eyes – unless it's a horror-western, maybe.

CAPITALIZING WORDS. Don't. Do not capitalize a word in any dialogue, like: 'NO! I absolutely REFUSE. NO!' That should be: '*No!* I absolutely refuse. *No!*' The italics are for emphasis. Capitalized text shouts – and sometimes it shouts: 'Amateur!'

Sure about that? If you're unsure about a word, don't rely only on your spellcheck; refer to your dictionary. If in doubt, leave it out.

15

Synopsis and Blurb

The book's finished. Now comes the pitch to sell it. This is where the synopsis is important. And yet it often taxes the writer most.

Many writers claim they find a synopsis harder to write than the actual book!

Condense all those words in the book into about a page or two of synopsis?

No easy task. Remember, the synopsis doesn't hold back anything. You have to divulge the ending. Nobody's going to steal the idea. So, you can't really get away with 'and with one bound the sheriff overcame the villain.' The publisher/agent needs to know *how* the hero triumphed – hopefully using his skill and courage, both already outlined in the synopsis.

Note that a synopsis is usually written in the present tense, like film script narrative.

The synopsis for *The $300 Man* ran to 999 words, under two pages:

SYNOPSIS OF
THE $300 MAN by Ross Morton

Half-Mexican Corbin Molina is one of several train passengers being robbed by Bert and Elijah Granger. Corbin has no left hand, only a hook; he uses this to incapacitate one robber and shoots the second man. Corbin is feted as a hero, which sits badly with him as he prefers anonymity. On arrival at the town of Retribution, the bodies are handed over to Sheriff Deshler, who pays Corbin the bounty. Deshler warns Corbin there's a third Granger brother, Arnie, who might come gunning after him.

Corbin is more concerned with visiting the town's bordello. He's looking for a woman called Jean. While he's talking to the madam, they hear a scream and Corbin races upstairs to rescue Jean from a crazy knifeman. Jean is his girlfriend of twelve years ago, before he went to fight for the Union in the Civil War.

He'd lied about his age and was paid $300 by his friend Sam Buford to act as Sam's substitute in the draft. Jean then reveals that during the war Sam's pa died and the Buford family sold up; Sam took Jean as his girlfriend – until they got to Retribution where she was sold into prostitution at Ma Begley's. She was ill treated by Ma's sons, Rufus and Mort, who later ran off.

Corbin buys Jean's freedom. His destination is Walkerville, a town renamed after the philanthropic Walker family turned up. Walkerville's shopkeepers are cowed by Walker's men. A homestead family, the Pikes, are driven out by McLaughlin, Rufus and Mort.

Just before leaving Retribution on the stage, Corbin is confronted by the town drunk, Jeremiah. He manages to defuse the situation and befriends Jeremiah, giving him advice and money to go sober. Joining Corbin in the stage is Tillman, a gunslinger.

Some time after the stage has left Retribution, Sheriff Deshler encounters the third Granger brother, Arnie. Before he can arrest him, he's shot in the back by Stella Granger. The pair learn that the killer of their brothers is Corbin Molina and that he's on the stage. They set out to ambush Corbin.

Meanwhile, Jeremiah accosts Jean, who is leaving town at last, and accompanies her to Walkerville.

It's clear that Mr Walker is dominated by his mother. She's a scheming woman who can twist the mayor round her little finger. Walker takes his mother's guidance and dominates the town; he arranged for an explosion in the silver mine, which is owned by the local Don; two Mexican workers were injured and are taken to the town's sawbones, Dr Malinda Dix. Sheriff Clegg has a crush on the doctor – but he's also in Walker's pocket.

Finally, now that the Pikes are far enough away from Walkerville, McLaughlin and his men cold-bloodedly murder the Pike family, making it look like a robbery.

During the night stop at a stage station, Corbin is threatened by Arnie – but disarms him. Tillman saves Corbin from being shot in the back by Stella. Next day, on their way, they discover the murdered Pike family.

On arrival at Walkerville, they inform Sheriff Clegg what happened. Tillman goes off to chat with Mr Walker – he's not pleased since he'd come to be the town's sheriff... Walker wants Tillman to kill Clegg and replace him. Tillman agrees, providing he can arrange it to appear legal.

Tillman's chance comes earlier than he'd thought. That evening he spots Sheriff Clegg assaulting Doctor Dix. Clegg is shot but not killed: the doctor's presence is crucial.

Next morning, Corbin goes to the sheriff's office to explain why he's in town – and is surprised to find Tillman is the new lawman. Corbin gives Tillman a letter from the head of the Ministry of the Interior Board of Reconstruction. Corbin's a Special Marshal tasked with rooting out corruption and thieving by northerners preying on the defeated poor southerners. There's a flashback to Major Newton giving Corbin the job; in the five years since, Corbin has tamed a number of towns in the south and rid them of opportunists and carpetbaggers.

Corbin starts questioning the townspeople, the general store owner, the barber and the cobbler. On seeing the doctor's shingle, he remembers. He was in the thick of the fighting at Wilmington, attempting to take Fort Fisher at the end of the war. He saved Major Newton and in the process his hand was seriously damaged and was amputated by Doctor Malinda Dix. During his convalescence, Malinda and Corbin get to know each other, both having a taste for poetry – he, Walt Whitman, she Christina Rossetti.

Corbin continues with his questioning of the townspeople. He talks to the freedmen and the Mexicans, building a damning indictment against the Walkers.

Tillman links the murder of the Pikes to two Walker men and the showdown ends in their death. Corbin encounters the Begley brothers and defeats them in a gun battle.

That evening, McLaughlin and the Walker men burst in to Corbin's room during Corbin's passionate moments with Malinda. They take them both to the mine, where Corbin learns that the Walkers had changed their name from Buford. Sam was his old pal, the man he'd substituted in the war. They are going to be blown up with the Mexican Don – but then Mrs Walker realises Corbin's report isn't in his belongings...

There's another paragraph to follow, but that's the critical ending, so I'm not including it here. Yes, I put in the confrontation, who dies and the revelations about Sam and Corbin's past.

Much of what was used in the synopsis was gleaned from several chunks of character backstory, and bits of the plot-plan, duly honed down to barely pertinent facts that move the story forward. I've tried to show the interaction between the different characters, too.

Normally, a synopsis doesn't allow for much character description – actions speak. What a person does reveals character.

And a blurb – in only about 300 words?

If the synopsis is difficult, imagine how hard a book blurb must be! You thought the publisher wrote the blurb? Some do, and will as a last resort if the author can't supply a suitable version. But really the author should do it, since the author knows the book better than anyone else. So, be prepared to write a blurb.

The blurb is the sales pitch, if you like, beckoning the reader to take a look between the book covers. It's written in the present tense too.

As you're restricted to a relatively few words – to fit on to the back cover or dust-jacket flyleaf, you can't go into the whys and wherefores. You have to introduce the main characters only, there's no room for the entire cast. And there must be action, and a threat. And here you most certainly don't give away too much, and most definitely not the ending!

The best way to prepare for writing the blurb is to read several from your book collection. Scan the Internet. Get a feel for the style.

Here's an example:

The $300 Man – the blurb
What's a life worth? $300, maybe.

Half-Mexican Corbin Molina lost a hand during the Civil War but he has adapted. Now he's on a mission to Walkerville. On the way, he prevents a train robbery and finds an old friend. Corbin always carries $300, which is significant, since that's what he was paid as a substitute soldier for the Union.

When Corbin starts asking questions about Walkerville's law and administration, he discovers that the Walker family, who seem to have bought and paid for loyalty and position, dominates the townspeople.

Inevitably, Corbin's questions attract plenty of trouble. And his past emerges to confront him during a tense showdown that threatens not only him but also his newfound love.

There's no scope to mention Jean, save that she's the 'old friend'. I don't dwell on their past or the sheriff of Retribution or even the serious threat the Granger family pose. There's no room to mention the gunslinger Tillman, either. Malinda is deliberately not named, as I didn't want to give away too much, so she simply becomes a 'newfound love', though that's cheating a little since it was a love he found again.

Find out what the core of the novel is about – in Corbin Molina's case, it's his mission to root out corruption – even at the risk of his heart. Yes, maybe the theme of the book will be adequate to use for the blurb.

The blurb has to end on a note of concern, teasing the reader to find out how the hero – or heroine – will overcome the pressing dilemma.

Ready to send your baby into the world?

You've done all you can now. Written the book, self-edited it, prepared a synopsis and even a blurb, which might be useful in the query letter.

All that work – and now you have to convince somebody not only to read it, but also to buy it. To do that, you need a query letter.

16

Marketing

Query Letter

This is the query letter for my first western, way back in 2007. Once I'd become a Hale author, the query letter didn't have to go for a sales pitch. They knew I could write. They still needed the text and the synopsis to read.

Dear Mr Hale
BLACK HORSE WESTERN SUBMISSION –
DEATH AT BETHESDA FALLS

Please find enclosed the first three chapters and a synopsis for the above titled western, which follows your guidelines.

Over the years, I've written and sold in excess of 60 short stories to magazines and am currently the contributing chief sub-editor of a monthly colour magazine, *The Portsmouth and District Post*, which I accomplish via Broadband here in Spain. I also write a monthly crime story and reviews and articles for *The Coastal Press*, an English language monthly magazine in Spain.

I was the finalist in the World One Day Novel Writing competition and my novella was praised by Terry Pratchett and Melvyn Bragg. A number of my short stories have won awards and been published in hardback and paperback anthologies. Last year I was joint runner-up in the Harry Bowling Prize novel competition with a crime thriller.

Would you be interested in seeing the full manuscript of DEATH AT BETHESDA FALLS?

An IRC is attached for a response or alternatively please reply by e-mail. The manuscript pages are disposable and can be recycled.

Yours sincerely,

[Since then my short story publication count is about 120 and I've had 15 books published.]

Things to avoid in your query letter

Don't ramble on and insert four pages about the book. Query letters should be brief, ideally one page; two at maximum.

Don't tell the publisher that your mother/sister/best friend says it's better than Elmore Leonard. The book has to speak for itself. Of course, if you know a published author who can endorse your book, mention it and offer a quotation.

Don't tell the publisher that you're not sure about how to approach him, but would he mind having a look at your story? This suggests you're an amateur who hasn't read any guides on writing or subscribed to any writing magazines.

Don't tell the publisher anything about yourself or career that is not pertinent to the novel. If the book is about a saloon in Topeka, and you've been working as a croupier in Manchester, then okay, it's pertinent, perhaps.

Don't neglect the SAE if you're approaching by snail mail. No SAE means no response; your postage, the printing, the paper – all wasted.

Don't ignore the publisher's requirements, maybe by stating, 'I haven't got time to format the book as you want it. It's a waste of my creativity. Besides, it's a creative expression as it is.' [Yes, I've received something along those lines before, believe me!]

Conclusion

Nobody ever pretended that writing a book of any length would be easy. But it can be done. And it can be done in thirty days, if you stick to the schedule.

I wish you the best of luck, not only with writing the book, but discovering the fascinating world of the western.

Bear in mind that, no matter how much effort you put into the book, it might be luck in the end that swings your way.

There's always room for more writers of westerns.

So, mount up and ride out!

Appendices

A. 30-day countdown

It's quite possible a lot of readers will turn to this section first, expecting some magic method to get those words down on the page or screen.

As I've said already, there is no magic method – just self-discipline and perseverance.

Remember, each 'day' amounts to a total of 8 hours' work.

A breakdown of the schedule might be as follows:

Day 1

Decide on location and date of story

Write plot-plan

Create main characters

Day 2

Build characters

Flesh out plot-plan now I know the characters better

Day 3

Start the story

Write 1,800 words

Monitor total words at end of day

Days 4–27

Write 1,800 words per day

Monitor total words at the end of each day

Day 28

Total words so far = 43,200

Write 1,800 words or so and *finish* novel. This is the *first draft*.

Count total words of novel

Day 29

Self-edit critically, create a *second draft*, and maybe a *third*, which will entail writing more words, and probably getting rid of others

Count total words of novel – it should still be in the ballpark of 45,000

Day 30

Assess chapters, structure, and do *final self-edit*

Write blurb

Write synopsis

Write letter to publisher

That might work.

But there will be days when tinkering slows you down and you only manage a few hundred new words. At other times, as the narrative flow has you in its grip, the words might be in the region of 3,500 for that session/day.

For *The $300 Man*, in a good day I managed 3,853, while on a slow day I only wrote 34 words (but I did a lot of self-editing and restructuring in those eight hours).

Whatever the number of words, keep track of what is left to attain your goal.

That goal creates the impetus to keep typing.

B. Word count

While most publishers are quite happy to accept the word count provided by your computer, a few may have a different requirement. It should be obvious from their website what they need.

A case in point is Robert Hale, whose word count requirement is not based on the computer word count. That's because all of their hardback westerns are 160 pages long. They have scope to juggle with a reasonably broad band of total words by changing the size of type, spacing the chapters etc.

The method for word count from Robert Hale Ltd is as follows:

CALCULATION OF LENGTH OF TYPESCRIPTS

The purpose of calculating the wordage of any typescript is to determine the number of printed pages it will occupy. The precise word count is of *no* use since it tells nothing about the number of short lines resulting from paragraphing or dialogue (particularly important with fiction).

Calculation is therefore based on the assumption that all printed pages have no paragraph beginnings or endings and the type area is completely filled with words.

To assess the wordage, proceed as follows:

1 Ensure the typewriting is the same throughout in terms of size, length of line etc. If not the procedure given below should be followed separately for each individual style of typing and the results added together.

2 Count 50 full-length lines and find the average number of words – e.g. 50 lines of 560 words gives an average of 11.2 words.

3 Average the number of lines over 10 characteristic pages – e.g. 245 lines on 10 pages gives an average of 24.5 lines.

4 Multiply the averages of 2 and 3 to get an average per page – e.g. 11.2 x 24.5 = 274.

5 Ensure the page numbering is consecutive then multiply the word average per page by the number of pages (count short pages at beginnings and ends of chapters as full pages).

6 Draw attention to, but do not count, foreword, preface, introduction, bibliography, appendices, index, maps or other line figures.

There is ample leeway, as it happens.

For my westerns accepted by Hale, my word counts have been:

Death at Bethesda Falls – computer count, 34,500
Last Chance Saloon – computer count, 39,900
The $300 Man – computer count, 39,900

Blind Justice at Wedlock – computer count, 38,300
Old Guns – computer count, 37,200

All of the above computer word counts amount to anywhere from 43,000 to 47,000 by the above Hale word counting method.

C. Publishers and Literary Agents

Publishers

The financial climate and the constant business restructuring that seems endemic continue to whittle away at traditional and new publishers. The following listing of publishers of western fiction is accurate at time of going to press. Check the respective websites for up-to-date information.

Robert Hale

http://www.halebooks.com

Hale has been around since 1936, one of the last bastions of independent publishing in the UK. They do consider unsolicited manuscripts for publication.

Send Robert Hale submissions to:

Editorial Department
Robert Hale Limited
Clerkenwell House
45/47 Clerkenwell Green
London EC1R 0HT

If your material is unsolicited, send three sample chapters and a synopsis in the first instance.

If you wish your typescript/sample material to be returned to you, enclose a self-addressed envelope with the appropriate return postage. This can be in stamp, cheque or postal order form. Robert Hale Limited reserves the right to dispose of typescripts within three months if appropriate postage is not forthcoming.

Hale's guidelines for their westerns are:

- 45,000 words is the ideal length (but see Appendix B for word count process)
- Authentic background and detail essential
- Strong sympathetic central figure/hero
- Little or no sex or undue violence
- Strong storyline with suspense and action
- Happy or at least conclusive ending
- Best written in straightforward English (not American) and a minimum of phonetic dialogue

Avalon Books

http://avalonbooks.com/index.php/writer-guidelines

Avalon Books imprint publishes hardcover westerns focussing primarily on the library market. There is *no* explicit sexual content or profanity in their novels. They publish 12 westerns a year in bimonthly cycles of two.

Book length: from a minimum of 50,000 words to a maximum of 70,000 words.

"All Westerns are historical novels. It is important that characters and setting be placed in time and that the background is carefully researched. Avoid using words and phrases that were not part of the language at the time your Western is set. Though it is important for flavor and authenticity to use some Westernisms in dialogue, overuse of dialect is to be avoided. Plots should be suspenseful and action packed. Stereotypes are to be avoided."

"The hero must be a strong individual with sound values. He's excellent with his fists and his gun, but not overeager to use either."

Avalon accepts unagented material. They require a query letter that briefly introduces your story, the genre (western), and your manuscript's total word count. Also include a 2–3 page (and no longer) synopsis of the entire manuscript and the first three chapters. All submissions must be typed and double spaced. The length of time for response to a query may vary from a week to a few months. If they ask for the full manuscript, the review times are approximately 10–12 months based on publication needs.

Queries that do not include an SASE will not be answered. If any of the above guidelines are not met your submission may not be reviewed. The *only exception* to the SASE rule is for authors living outside of the United States; but make sure to include a valid e-mail address so that Avalon may respond to your query.

Avalon is not accepting e-mail queries at this time.

The address for submissions:

The Editors

Avalon Books

1202 Lexington Avenue, Ste. 283,

New York, NY 10028

Western Trail Blazer

http://westerntrailblazer.com/submission-guidelines.php

Send a query which includes author name; website or blog link (if available); genre, heat rating (Adult, General, Young Adult), length of story; and a brief description of the manuscript (should be no longer than two or three paragraphs). Do not submit your manuscript or any attachments unless requested. Send your query to: booksbyrebecca@yahoo.com

If a manuscript is requested, submit only a complete Submission Ready (see website) manuscript as an attachment. What Western Trail Blazer are looking for:

Traditional Westerns

Historical Westerns, Civil War, and Exploration (as long as Western Elements are a major part of the theme)

Westerns with Romantic Elements

Paranormal Westerns (includes Contemporary Ranch or Native American stories)

Spooky Westerns (must be Western themed)

Time Travel Westerns (must be Western themed and may contain romantic element)

Humour-Satire (can be contemporary but must relate to a Western character).

Prizm Books

www.prizmbooks.com

Publishes Young Adult westerns (written for ages 12 and up).

All manuscripts must be submitted to submissions@prizmbooks.com as an attachment in either .doc, .txt, or .rtf format.

Length of manuscript requirement:

Novel – 45,000 words and up (e-books & print)

Novella – 20–45,000 words (e-book only)

Novelette – 10–20,000 words (e-book only)

Short Stories – Under 10,000 words (e-book only)

All submissions must be spellchecked, edited for grammar and be single spaced with a space in between paragraphs. Indents at the beginning of paragraphs are not necessary. *Note the special requirements here!* Any submissions with severe formatting problems (i.e.: blocks of text with no paragraph breaks, illegible fonts) will not be read.

Include a word count and a brief synopsis of the work.

All spelling should be in American English

See the website for full requirements, however.

Bethany House

http://www.bethanyhouse.com

Publisher of Christian Western fiction. An imprint of Baker Books, Bethany House will consider unsolicited work only through one of the following avenues. Materials sent to their editorial staff through a professional literary agent will be considered; in addition, their staff attends various writers' conferences at which prospective authors can develop relationships with those in the publishing industry. You may also submit your work to one or both of the manuscript submission services Authonomy.com and Christian Manuscript Submissions, an online service of the Evangelical Christian Publishers' Association. These organizations serve as liaisons between publishers and prospective authors.

Barbarian Books

http://www.barbarianbooks.com

Small press e-book publisher of Westerns (including cross-genre). Pays 70% royalties. Does not charge authors any fees. No print runs. Length required: Novel, from 60,000 to 105,000 words. (If it's close, send it.)

Whiskey Creek Press

http://www.whiskeycreekpress.com

Whiskey Creek Press is a royalty-paying traditional publisher of fiction and non-fiction, and publishes in e-book and trade paperback formats. They're always open for submissions. Whiskey Creek Press charges no fees of any kind to authors for publishing services.

Manuscript length should be at least 50,000 words; they prefer works in the 60,000–80,000 range but will consider manuscripts up to 100,000 words.

Send: a) A cover letter outlining your manuscript, any past publications and experiences as a writer. In the cover letter, include the word length of your manuscript as well as a brief synopsis, one to two pages in length. Summarize the beginning, middle and end of the story. Show the conflict and resolution as well as character description. Also include a one-paragraph synopsis (thumbnail sketch or 'blurb') of the story line and tell them what motivated you to write this story. Provide any past publishing history in detail, including books under contract with other publishers and titles out of print. b) A business plan, typically one page in length, detailing how you will promote and market your published manuscript, including any past marketing efforts for your writing career. Do you have a current author website? If so, include that, along with any other sites like MySpace, Yahoo, and so forth that you use to market your works. An active author website is mandatory for all WCP authors. c) The *completed* manuscript. Do not send a few chapters. Do not mail the manuscript. To preserve the beautiful Cottonwood trees growing along the banks of Whiskey Creek, they only accept submissions electronically. E-mail your completed submission package to: subs@whiskeycreekpress.com.

Solstice Publishing

www.solsticepublishing.com

Publishes Solstice Westerns, books over 50,000 words, in e-book and print format. Their requirements:

1 Your query letter should be in the body of the initial e-mail and should include the blurb for the manuscript. Also attached should be the original manuscript and a two to three page synopsis of your book.
2 Solstice will consider previously published work only if such work has been out of print for no less that one (1) year.
3 Manuscripts are reviewed on a monthly basis. You will receive confirmation of receipt at the time that your manuscript moves into the queue.

In addition, please observe the following formatting require-ments:

- All documents should be submitted in .doc, .docx, or .rtf format

- 12 pt. black font
- One inch margins throughout
- Single spacing between sentences
- No double returns between paragraphs (i.e. No spaces between paragraphs)
- Indent new paragraph using word processor settings – not with the tab key or space bar
- Use page breaks between chapters
- Italics, not underlining

You will hear back from Solstice usually within 3–6 weeks.

Berkley Books

www.us.penguingroup.com

Part of the massive Penguin Books conglomerate, USA. You need an agent to approach this publisher. The Signet imprint is also part of Penguin USA.

Literary Agents

Sadly, it seems that some literary agents are here one day and gone the next. Avoid questionable literary agencies; query agencies that have verifiable track records of sales to commercial publishing houses. How do you know they're questionable? Google 'worst literary agents'.

One option is to check with Agent Query online (http://www.agentquery.com), where the following were obtained; select fiction/western in the search box:

Aaron Priest Literary Agency
Cherry Weiner Literary Agency
Talcott Notch Literary Services
Schiavone Literary Agency
3 Seas Literary Agency
International Transactions
Rees Literary Agency

Donald Maass Literary Agency
McGinniss Associates Literary Agency

D. Formatting the manuscript

Most publishers will give you guidelines on their websites. Ignore their guidelines at your peril. If you can't be bothered to adhere to their request, why should they bother to look at your submission?

It sometimes matters whether your target is a US publisher or a British one. Usually, British opt for the single quote mark (') for speech, while the US prefer the double quotes (").

While Internet set-up seems to have adopted no paragraph indents and a space between paragraphs for ease of on-screen reading, this is *not* normal for a manuscript, even if sent as an attachment via e-mail – paragraphs should be indented.

Freelance Writing – Presentation – How To Submit Your Work

Normal format

The normal standard for presentation of your manuscript is as outlined below. (At the risk of bringing to mind grannies and egg-sucking, some computer cues are also offered.) Online submissions – same applies, save there's no printing or envelopes!

Cover sheet to include:
Name
Address
Phone number
E-mail address
Title
By-line (i.e. penname or name you wish to use)
Word count
… and anything else required by a publisher's guidelines

Top of all pages to contain (View/Header and footer/*then type in…*):

title

page number (Insert/Page numbers/format/start at – type in 0; *this means that the cover sheet will be 0 and your first page will be page* 1)

name

Typed/computer printed:

in black only, no fancy colours

restrict typeface to Times Roman or New Courier 12 pt.

Double-spaced lines (Format/Paragraph/line spacing – *select Double*)

Indent paragraphs (Format/Tabs/*change default tab stops to 0.5cm or 0.9cm appropriate*)

No extra spaces for new paragraphs

Use quotation marks for speech (*don't* emulate prize-winner Cormac McCarthy!)

Do not align text on the right – the right-hand side should appear ragged.

Print single side of paper

Collate and *check* that all pages are in the correct order

Do not staple or otherwise fix the pages together

Do not insert in a folder

Type covering letter

Insert manuscript and covering letter in envelope

Size of envelope: Use A4 size envelope; bulky manuscripts/ novels, use padded type.

Insert SAE if you want the manuscript returned; as postage is costly, the alternative is to mention in the query letter that the manuscript is disposable and the SAE is simply for a reply. (You have to weigh up the cost of ink/paper against postage.)

What to send in the first instance.

The first three chapters and synopsis. Check with online guidelines, if available, or *The Writer's Handbook*. Some publishers are happy to accept the whole manuscript, especially if it's an attachment via e-mail.

E. Western Fiction book list

A selection of authors and their western fiction, by no means exhaustive:

Baker, Madeline	*Apache Runaway; Cheyenne Surrender*
Ballas, Jack	*Gun Boss; Powder River; Tomahawk Canyon; Maverick Guns*
Berger, Thomas	*Little Big Man*
Bishop, Pike	*Diamondback: Shroud of Vengeance*
Blake, Michael	*Dances with Wolves; The Holy Road*
Blevins, Win	*Stone Song*
Boggs, Johnny D.	*West Texas Kill; The Killing Shot; Walk Proud, Stand Tall*
Brand, Max	*The Trail to San Triste; The Outlaw of Buffalo Flat; Ambush at Torture Canyon; Cheyenne Gold; Shotgun Law; Six-Gun Country; Destry Rides Again*
Brandvold, Peter	*Bullets Over Bedlam; Dust of the Damned*
Brandt, Lyle	*Lawman: Hanging Judge; Lawman: Manhunt*
Braun, Matt	*Wyatt Earp; The Kincaids; Wages of Sin*
Bridges, Ben	*Draw Down the Lightning; Thunder Gorge; Blood Canyon; Wilde Fire; Silver Trail*
Brown, Dee	*Creek Mary's Blood; Killdeer Mountain*
Burns, Terry	*The Sagebrush Collection*

Cameron, Marc	*Hard Road to Heaven; The Hell Riders*
Carter, Forrest	*Watch for Me on the Mountain; The Outlaw Josey Wales*
Catha, Willa	*O Pioneers!*
Chamberlain, Daniel C.	*The Long Shooters*
Charlier & Moebius	*Blueberry (graphic novel series)*
Christian, Frederick H.	*Sudden Strikes Back; Sudden at Bay*
Clark, Steven	*The Guerrilla Man: Bloody Trail to Kansas*
Clark, Walter Van Tilburg	*The Ox-Bow Incident*
Compton, Ralph	*The Goodnight Trail; The Western Trail; The Chisholm Trail*
Cook, John Byrne	*The Snowblind Moon*
Cotton, Tell	*Confessions of a Gunfighter*
Cranmer, David	*Cash Laramie series*
Crider, Bill	*Galveston Gunman; A Time for Hanging; Texas Vigilante*
Dailey, Janet	*The Pride of Hannah Wade*
Deane, Mike	*Wagon Hunt; Drive to Redemption*
Dobbins, Brian	*Corryville*
Douglas, Jake	*Silent Wolf; Halfway to Hell; Sound of Gunfire; Judas Pass; Laredo's Land*
Dunlap, Phil	*Saving Mattie; Cotton's War*
Edson, J.T.	*The Fortune Hunters; Guns in the Night; Terror Valley; Cold Deck, Hot Lead; The Town Tamers*
Eidson, Thomas	*Hannah's Gift; The Last Ride; St. Agnes' Stand*
Estleman, Loren D.	*Journey of the Dead; Sudden Country*
Ferber, Edna	*Cimarron*

Fergus, Jim	*One Thousand White Women*
Fisher, Dave P.	*Bitter Grass; Bronc Buster*
Flynn, T.T.	*The Man from Laramie*
Fraser, George MacDonald	*Flashman and the Redskins*
Giles, Jack	*Lawmen; The Fourth Horseman; Rebel Run*
Gilman, George G.	*Edge: The Loner; Adam Steele 1: The Violent Peace*
Grey, Zane	*Riders of the Purple Sage; The Lone Star Ranger*
Griffin, James J.	*Death Rides the Rails*
Guin, Jerry	*Trail Dust*
Guthrie, A.B.	*The Big Sky; The Way West*
Harrison, D.M.	*The Buffalo Soldier; Going to See the Elephant*
Harte, Bret	*The Story of a Mine and Other Tales*
Henry, O.	*The Heart of the West*
Henry, Will	*The Gates of the Mountains; MacKenna's Gold; Reckoning at Yankee Flat; The Last Warpath*
Herzberg, Bob	*Quantrill's Gold*
Hill, Ruth Beebe	*Hanta Yo*
Hirt, Douglas	*The Silent Gun; Ketcham's Land; Colorado Gold*
Howard, Lance	*Blood Pass; Nightmare Pass; The Comanche's Ghost; The Silver-mine Spook; The Phantom Marshal*
Jackson, Dale B.	*They Rode Good Horses; Unbroke Horses*
James, Terry	*Long Shadows*
Johnson, Dorothy Marie	*Indian Country*

Johnston, Terry C.	*Sioux Dawn; Red Cloud's Revenge; Carry the Wind*
Johnston, William W.	*The Last Mountain Man; Eyes of Eagles*
Joyner, C. Courtney	*Tracking the Devil*
Kelton, Elmer	*The Time It Never Rained; The Far Canyon; Texas Sunrise*
L'Amour, Louis	*Flint; Hondo; The Outlaws of Mesquite; The Cherokee Trail; The Ferguson Rifle; How the West Was Won; Sackett's Land; Bowdrie; Shalako; Showdown at Yellow Butte*
Latham, Aaron	*Code of the West*
Legg, John	*To Face a Savage Land; Buckskin Vengeance*
Leigh, Joanne	*Almost a Stranger*
LeMay, Alan	*The Searchers; The Unforgiven*
Leonard, Elmore	*Hombre; Valdez is Coming; Last Stand at Saber River*
Logan, Matt	*Coffin Creek; Tanner's Guns*
Loveday, John	*Halo*
Lowrance, Heath	*Miles to Little Ridge*
MacLean, Alistair	*Breakheart Pass*
Martin, George R.R.	*Fevre Dream*
Martin, Jack	*The Tarnished Star; Arkansas Smith; The Ballad of Delta Rose*
Martin, L.J.	*Shadow of the Grizzly; Shadow of the Mast*
Masero, Tony	*Jake Rains; The Riflemen; The Pursued*
Masterton, Graham	*Empress*

Mayo, Matthew P.	*Winter's War; Wrong Town; Hot Lead, Cold Heart*
McCarthy, Cormac	*Blood Meridian*
McCarthy, Gary	*Powder River; Wind River*
McMurtry, Larry	*Lonesome Dove; Buffalo Girls; Comanche Moon; Dead Man's Walk; Streets of Laredo*
Michener, James A.	*Centennial; Texas*
Miller, Rod	*Gallows for a Gunman*
Mims, Meg	*Double Crossing*
More, Clay	*Stampede at Rattlesnake Pass; Nemesis for the Judge*
Morton, Ross	*Last Chance Saloon; Blind Justice at Wedlock; Old Guns*
Nesbitt, John D.	*Gather My Horses; Stranger in Thunder Basin*
Nevin, David	*DreamWest*
O'Keefe, Chap	*Blast to Oblivion; The Gunman and the Actress; The Outlaw and the Lady; The Sheriff and the Widow; Doomsday Mesa; Misfit Lil Rides In*
Oke, Janette	*Love Comes Softly; Love's Enduring Promise; Love Finds a Home; A Gown of Spanish Lace*
Olsen, T.V.	*A Killer is Waiting; The Stalking Moon; Arrow in the Sun*
Overholser, Wayne D.	*Red is the Valley; Valley of Guns*
Paine, Lauran	*Border Town; The Killer Gun; The Dark Trail; The Open Range Men*
Parker, Robert B.	*Appaloosa; Resolution; Brimstone; Blue-Eyed Devil*

Parnham, Ian	*Bad Moon Over Devil's Ridge; Calloway's Crossing; Six-shooter Bride; Dead by Sundown; The Outlawed Deputy*
Peterson, Pete	*The Relentless Gun; A Dark Trail Winding*
Pierson, Cheryl	*Fire Eyes*
Portis, Charles	*True Grit*
Prate, Kit	*Long Ride to Limbo; Miss Annie; Sharpshooter*
Pronzini, Bill	*The Last Days of Horse-Shy Halloran; Starvation Camp; Firewind*
Proulx, Annie	*Close Range: Wyoming Stories*
Randisi, Robert J.	*Gunsmith series; Bounty series; Mountain Man Jack series*
Reasoner, James	*Wind River; Redemption series; Manassas; Shiloh etc.*
Richards, Dusty	*The Sundown Chaser*
Richter, Conrad	*The Sea of Grass*
Rizzo, Tom	*Last Stand at Bitter Creek*
Robson, Lucia St Clair	*Ride the Wind; Walk in My Soul*
Rockfern, Daniel	*Duel at Cheyenne; Long Ride into Hell*
Roderus, Frank	*The Outsider; Hell Creek Cabin; Leaving Kansas; Reaching Colorado; Finding Nevada*
Rogers, Jacquie	*Much Ado About Marshals*
Ross, David William	*Beyond the Stars*
Russell, Allen	*Crow Feather*
Sanders, D.F.	*Heart of the Land*
Sanders, J.R.	*The Littlest Wrangler*
Satterthwait, Walter	*Wilde West*

Schaefer, Jack	*Shane; Monte Walsh; The Big Range*
Sherman, Jory	*The Medicine Horn; The Dark Land; Savage Vengeance*
Short, Luke	*Vengeance Valley; Donovan's Gun*
Smiley, Jane	*The All-True Travels and Adventures of Lidie Newton*
Smith, Troy D.	*Blackwell's Star; Blackwell's Stand*
Spellman, Cathy Cash	*Paint the Wind*
Strange, Oliver	*The Range Robbers; Sudden etc.*
Swarthout, Glendon	*The Shootist; The Homesman*
Sweazy, Larry	*The Cougar's Prey; The Scorpion Trail*
Taylor, Gillian F.	*Silver Express; Two-Gun Trouble; Navajo Rock; San Felipe Guns; Hyde's Honour*
Thompson, David	*Wilderness: King of the Mountain*
Thompson, E.V.	*Cry Once Alone; No Less Than the Journey*
Tyrell, Chuck	*Hell Fire in Paradise; Vulture Gold; The Snake Den; Trail of a Hard Man; Guns of Ponderosa; Return to Silver Creek*
Van Pelt, Lori	*Pecker's Revenge and Other Stories from the Frontier's Edge*
Vardeman, Robert	*Slocum series; Sonora Noose*
Vaughan, Robert	*Hawke series; Wild Wild West series; Range Wars*
Washburn, L.J.	*Bandera Pass; Ghost River*
Wellman, Paul I.	*Death on the Prairie*
West, Joseph A.	*Johnny Blue and the Hanging Judge*
Whitehead, David	*Cougar Valley; Heller in the Rockies; Law of the Gun*

Wiktorek, Adam W.	*Mead's Quest*
Wildey, Doug	*Rio; Rio Rides Again graphic novels*
Williamson, Penelope	*Heart of the West*
Willman, Marianne	*Pieces of Sky*
Wister, Owen	*The Virginian*
Woolard, James R.	*Thunder in the Valley; Blood at Dawn; Colorado Sam*

F. Selection of western series characters

The series character is shown in capital letters. Some of the authors of these series will have more than one penname, they're that prolific! For example, Ben Bridges is the penname of David Whitehead, who also uses Matt Logan, Glenn Lockwood and Carter West. A comprehensive list can be found at Steve Myall's Western Fiction Review blog. There are actually many more excellent series than listed here!

ALLISON, Jim by Ben Bridges – 3 books
BENEDICT & BRAZOS by E. Jefferson Clay – 35+ books
BLADE by Matt Chisholm – 12 books
BLAKE, Faro by Zeke Masters – 31 books
BOLT by Cort Martin – 26 books
BURRACK, Sam by Ralph Cotton – 25+ books
CADE, Jubal by Charles R. Pike – 22 books
CHEYENNE by Judd Cole – 22+ books
CIVIL WAR BATTLES (The) by James Reasoner – 10 books
DILLARD by Chap O'Keefe – 9 books
DOC & RAIDER by J.D. Hardin – 73 books
EASY COMPANY by John Wesley Howard – 31 books
EDGE by George G. Gilman – 61 books
FARGO by John Benteen – 23 books
GOLDEN HAWK by Will C. Knott – 9 books
GRINGOS by J.D. Sandon – 10 books
GUNMAN'S REPUTATION by Ralph Cotton – 11+ books

GUNN by Jory Sherman – 29 books
GUNSLINGER by Charles G. Garrett – 10 books
GUNSMITH (The) by J.R. Roberts – 384+ books
HALFADAY CREEK by James B. Hendryx – 15 books
HALLIDAY by Adam Brady – 15+ books
HANGING JUDGE (The) by Jerome Gardner – 12+ books
HART THE REGULATOR by John B. Harvey – 10 books
HATFIELD, Jim by Jackson Cole – 80+ books
HENRY, Yakima by Frank Leslie – 9+ books
HERNE THE HUNTER by John J. McLaglen – 24 books
HEWITT, Jefferson by John Reese – 11 books
IRON EYES by Rory Black – 16+ books
JUSTICE, Ruff by Warren T. Longtree – 28 books
JUDGE (The) by Hank Edwards – 12 books
KANE, Morgan by Louis Masterson – 41 books in English (83 in Norwegian)
LONE STAR by Wesley Ellis – 153 books
LONG RIDER by Clay Dawson – 27 books
LASSITER by Jack Slade – 30 books
LONER (The) by J.A. Johnstone – 15 books
LAST GUNFIGHTER (The) by William W. Johnstone / J.A. Johnstone – 23 books
LONGARM by Tabor Evans – 430+ books
MOUNTAIN JACK PIKE by Joseph Meek – 15 books
McALLISTER by Matt Chisholm – 39 books
MOUNTAIN MAN (The) by William W. Johnstone / J.A. Johnstone – 39+ books
O'GRADY, Canyon by Jon Sharpe – 25 books
PLAINSMEN (The) by Terry C. Johnston – 16 books
RAMSEYS (The) by Will McLennan – 18 books
RAIDER by J.D. Hardin – 42 books
RIVERS WEST by various authors – 20 books
REGULATOR (The) by Dale Colter – 12 books
STEELE, Adam by George G. Gilman – 49 books

SEARCHER by Josh Edwards – 12 books

STRINGER by Lou Cameron – 15 books

SHELTER by Paul Ledd – 33 books

SLADE, Walt by Bradford Scott – 115 books

SPANISH BIT SAGA (The) by Don Coldsmith – 28 books

STAGECOACH by Hank Mitchum – 52 books

SCOUT (The) by Buck Gentry – 34 books

SUDDEN by Oliver Strange or Frederick H. Christian – 15 books

SPUR by Dirk Fletcher – 53+ books

SUNDANCE by John Benteen or Jack Slade or Peter McCurtin –
    43 books

SKYE's West by Richard S. Wheeler – 12 + books

SLOCUM by Jake Logan – 420+ books

TRAIL DRIVE by Ralph Compton – 22 + books

TRAILSMAN (The) by Jon Sharpe – 380+ books

WAGONS WEST by Dana Fuller Ross – 24 books

WHITE SQUAW by E.J. Hunter – 24 books

WILDERNESS by David Thompson – 73+ books

Index

**COMPASS
BOOKS**

Compass Books focuses on practical and informative 'how-to' books for writers. Written by experienced authors who also have extensive experience of tutoring at the most popular creative writing workshops, the books offer an insight into the more specialised niches of the publishing game.